THE
CORPUS
HERMETICUM

GRAND TYPE
GRANDTYPECLASSICS.COM

The Corpus Hermeticum
Trismegistus, Hermes

ISBN: 978-1-83412-272-4

THE CORPUS HERMETICUM

HERMES TRISMEGISTUS

Translation By
G. R. S. MEAD

GRAND TYPE CLASSICS

CONTENTS

The Corpus Hermeticum

CHAPTER ONE

Poemandres, the Shepherd of Men

NOTES ON THE TEXT: This is the most famous of the Hermetic documents, a revelation account describing a vision of the creation of the universe and the nature and fate of humanity. Authors from the Renaissance onward have been struck by the way in which its creation

myth seems partly inspired by Genesis, partly reacting against it. The Fall has here become the descent of the Primal Man through the spheres of the planets to the world of Nature, a descent caused not by disobedience but by love, and done with the blessing of God.

The seven rulers of fate discussed in sections 9, 14 and 25 are the archons of the seven planets, which also appear in Plato's Timaeus and in a number of the ancient writings usually lumped together as "Gnostic". Their role here is an oddly ambivalent one, powers of Harmony who are nonetheless the sources of humanity's tendencies to evil.

1. It chanced once on a time my mind was meditating on the things that are, my thought was raised to a great height, the senses of my body being held back - just as men who are weighed down with sleep after a fill of food, or from fatigue of body.

Methought a Being more than vast, in size beyond all bounds, called out my name and saith: What wouldst thou hear and see, and what hast thou in mind to learn and know?

2. And I do say: Who art thou?

He saith: I am Man-Shepherd (**Poemandres**), Mind of all-masterhood; I know what thou desirest and I am with thee everywhere.

3. [And] I reply: I long to learn the things that are, and comprehend their nature, and know God. This is, I said, what I desire to hear.

He answered back to me: Hold in thy mind all thou wouldst know, and I will teach thee.

4. Even with these words His aspect changed, and straightway, in the twinkling of an eye, all things were opened to me, and I see a Vision limitless, all things turned into Light - sweet, joyous [Light]. And I became transported as I gazed.

But in a little while Darkness came settling down on part [of it], awesome and gloomy, coiling in sinuous folds, so that methought it like unto a snake.

And then the Darkness changed into some sort of a Moist Nature, tossed about beyond all power of words, belching out smoke as from a fire, and groaning forth a wailing sound that beggars all description.

[And] after that an outcry inarticulate came forth from it, as though it were a Voice of Fire.

5. [Thereon] out of the Light [...] a Holy Word (Logos) descended on that Nature. And upwards to the height from the Moist Nature leaped forth pure Fire; light was it, swift and active too.

The Air, too, being light, followed after the Fire; from out of the Earth-and-Water rising up to Fire so that it seemed to hang therefrom.

But Earth-and-Water stayed so mingled with each other, that Earth from Water no one could discern. Yet were they moved to hear by reason of the Spirit-Word (Logos) pervading them.

6. Then saith to me Man-Shepherd: Didst understand this Vision what it means?

Nay; that shall I know, said I.

That Light, He said, am I, thy God, Mind, prior to Moist Nature which appeared from Darkness; the Light-Word (Logos) [that appeared] from Mind is Son of God.

What then? - say I.

Know that what sees in thee and hears is the Lord's Word (Logos); but Mind is Father-God. Not separate are they the one from other; just in their union [rather] is it Life consists.

Thanks be to Thee, I said.

So, understand the Light [He answered], and make friends with it.

7. And speaking thus He gazed for long into my eyes, so that I trembled at the look of him.

But when He raised His head, I see in Mind the Light, [but] now in Powers no man could number, and Cosmos grown beyond all bounds, and that the Fire was compassed round about by a most mighty Power, and [now] subdued had come unto a stand.

And when I saw these things I understood by reason of Man-Shepherd's Word (Logos).

8. But as I was in great astonishment, He saith to me again: Thou didst behold in Mind the Archetypal Form whose being is before beginning without end. Thus spake to me Man-Shepherd.

And I say: Whence then have Nature's elements their being?

To this He answer gives: From Will of God. [Nature] received the Word (Logos), and gazing upon the Cosmos Beautiful did copy it, making herself into a cosmos, by means of her own elements and by the births of souls.

9. And God-the-Mind, being male and female both, as Light and Life subsisting, brought forth another Mind to give things form, who, God as he was of Fire and Spirit, formed Seven Rulers who enclose the

cosmos that the sense perceives. Men call their ruling Fate.

10. Straightway from out the downward elements God's Reason (Logos) leaped up to Nature's pure formation, and was at-oned with the Formative Mind; for it was co-essential with it. And Nature's downward elements were thus left reason-less, so as to be pure matter.

11. Then the Formative Mind ([at-oned] with Reason), he who surrounds the spheres and spins them with his whorl, set turning his formations, and let them turn from a beginning boundless unto an endless end. For that the circulation of these [spheres] begins where it doth end, as Mind doth will.

And from the downward elements Nature brought forth lives reason-less; for He did not extend the Reason (Logos) [to them]. The Air brought forth things winged; the Water things that swim, and Earth-and-Water one from another parted, as Mind willed. And from her bosom Earth produced what lives she had, four-footed things and reptiles, beasts wild and tame.

12. But All-Father Mind, being Life and Light, did bring forth Man co-equal to Himself, with whom He fell in love, as being His own child; for he was beautiful beyond compare, the Image of his Sire. In very truth, God fell in love with his own Form; and on him did bestow all of His own formations.

13. And when he gazed upon what the Enformer had created in the Father, [Man] too wished to enform; and [so] assent was given him by the Father.

Changing his state to the formative sphere, in that he was to have his whole authority, he gazed upon his Brother's creatures. They fell in love with him, and gave him each a share of his own ordering.

And after that he had well learned their essence and had become a sharer in their nature, he had a mind to break right through the Boundary of their spheres, and to subdue the might of that which pressed upon the Fire.

14. So he who hath the whole authority over [all] the mortals in the cosmos and over its lives irrational, bent his face downwards through the Harmony, breaking right through its strength, and showed to downward Nature God's fair form.

And when she saw that Form of beauty which can never satiate, and him who [now] possessed within himself each single energy of [all seven] Rulers as well as God's own Form, she smiled with love; for it was as though she hadd seen the image of Man's fairest form upon her Water, his shadow on her Earth.

He in turn beholding the form like to himself, existing in her, in her Water, loved it and willed to live in it; and with the will came act, and [so] he vivified the form devoid of reason.

And Nature took the object of her love and wound herself completely around him, and they were intermingled, for they were lovers.

15. And this is why beyond all creatures

on the earth man is twofold; mortal because of body, but because of the essential man immortal.

Though deathless and possessed of sway over all, yet doth he suffer as a mortal doth, subject to Fate.

Thus though above the Harmony, within the Harmony he hath become a slave. Though male-female, as from a Father male-female, and though he is sleepless from a sleepless [Sire], yet is he overcome [by sleep].

16. Thereon [I say: Teach on], O Mind of me, for I myself as well am amorous of the Word (Logos).

The Shepherd said: This is the mystery kept hid until this day.

Nature embraced by Man brought forth a wonder, oh so wonderful. For as he had the nature of the Concord of the Seven, who, as I said to thee, [were made] of Fire and Spirit - Nature delayed not, but immediately brought forth seven "men", in correspondence with the natures of the Seven, male-female and moving in the air.

Thereon [I said]: O Shepherd, ..., for now I am filled with great desire and long to hear; do not run off.

The Shepherd said: Keep silence, for not as yet have I unrolled for thee the first discourse (logoi).

Lo! I am still, I said.

17. In such wise than, as I have said, the generation of these seven came to pass. Earth was as woman, her Water filled with longing; ripeness she took from Fire, spirit from Aether. Nature thus brought forth frames to suit the form of Man.

And Man from Light and Life changed into soul and mind - from Life to soul, from Light to mind.

And thus continued all the sense-world's parts until the period of their end and new beginnings.

18. Now listen to the rest of the discourse (Logos) which thou dost long to hear.

The period being ended, the bond that bound them all was loosened by God's Will. For all the animals being male-female, at the same time with Man were loosed apart; some became partly male, some in like fashion [partly] female. And straightway God spake by His Holy Word (Logos):

"Increase ye in increasing, and multiply in multitude, ye creatures and creations all; and man that hath Mind in him, let him learn to know that he himself is deathless, and that the cause of death is love, though Love is all."

19. When He said this, His Forethought did by means of Fate and Harmony effect their couplings and their generations founded. And so all things were multiplied according to their kind.

And he who thus hath learned to know himself, hath reached that Good which doth transcend abundance; but he who through a love that leads astray, expends his love upon his body - he stays in Darkness wandering, and suffering through his senses things of Death.

20. What is the so great fault, said I, the ignorant commit, that they should be deprived of deathlessness?

Thou seemest, He said, O thou, not to have given heed to what thou heardest. Did I not bid thee think?

Yea do I think, and I remember, and therefore give Thee thanks.

If thou didst think [thereon], [said He], tell me: Why do they merit death who are in Death?

It is because the gloomy Darkness is the root and base of the material frame; from it came the Moist Nature; from this the body in the sense-world was composed; and from this [body] Death doth the Water drain.

21. Right was thy thought, O thou! But how doth "he who knows himself, go unto Him", as God's Word (Logos) hath declared?

And I reply: the Father of the universals

doth consist of Light and Life, from Him Man was born.

Thou sayest well, [thus] speaking. Light and Life is Father-God, and from Him Man was born.

If then thou learnest that thou art thyself of Life and Light, and that thou [happenest] to be out of them, thou shalt return again to Life. Thus did Man-Shepherd speak.

But tell me further, Mind of me, I cried, how shall I come to Life again...for God doth say: "The man who hath Mind in him, let him learn to know that he himself [is deathless]."

22. Have not all men then Mind?

Thou sayest well, O thou, thus speaking. I, Mind, myself am present with holy men and good, the pure and merciful, men who live piously.

[To such] my presence doth become an aid, and straightway they gain gnosis of all things, and win the Father's love by their pure lives, and give Him thanks, invoking on Him blessings, and chanting hymns, intent on Him with ardent love.

And ere they give up the body unto its proper death, they turn them with disgust from its sensations, from knowledge of what things they operate. Nay, it is I, the Mind, that will not let the operations which befall the body, work to their [natural] end. For being door-keeper I will close up [all] the entrances, and cut the mental actions off which base and evil energies induce.

23. But to the Mind-less ones, the wicked and depraved, the envious and covetous, and those who mured do and love impiety, I am far off, yielding my place to the Avenging Daimon, who sharpening the fire, tormenteth him and addeth fire to fire upon him, and rusheth upon him through his senses, thus rendering him readier for transgressions of the law, so that he meets with greater torment; nor doth he ever cease to have desire for appetites inordinate, insatiately striving in the dark.

24. Well hast thou taught me all, as I desired,

O Mind. And now, pray, tell me further of the nature of the Way Above as now it is [for me].

To this Man-Shepherd said: When the material body is to be dissolved, first thou surrenderest the body by itself unto the work of change, and thus the form thou hadst doth vanish, and thou surrenderest thy way of life, void of its energy, unto the Daimon. The body's senses next pass back into their sources, becoming separate, and resurrect as energies; and passion and desire withdraw unto that nature which is void of reason.

25. And thus it is that man doth speed his way thereafter upwards through the Harmony.

To the first zone he gives the Energy of Growth and Waning; unto the second [zone], Device of Evils [now] de-energized; unto the third, the Guile of the Desires de-energized; unto the fourth, his Domineering Arrogance, [also] de-energized; unto the fifth, unholy Daring and the Rashness of

Audacity, de-energized; unto the sixth, Striving for Wealth by evil means, deprived of its aggrandizement; and to the seventh zone, Ensnaring Falsehood, de-energized.

26. And then, with all the energisings of the harmony stript from him, clothed in his proper Power, he cometh to that Nature which belongs unto the Eighth, and there with those-that-are hymneth the Father.

They who are there welcome his coming there with joy; and he, made like to them that sojourn there, doth further hear the Powers who are above the Nature that belongs unto the Eighth, singing their songs of praise to God in language of their own.

And then they, in a band, go to the Father home; of their own selves they make surrender of themselves to Powers, and [thus] becoming Powers they are in God. This the good end for those who have gained Gnosis - to be made one with God.

Why shouldst thou then delay? Must it not be, since thou hast all received, that thou shouldst to the worthy point the way, in order that through thee the race of mortal kind may by [thy] God be saved?

27. This when He had said, Man-Shepherd mingled with the Powers.

But I, with thanks and blessings unto the Father of the universal [Powers], was freed, full of the power he had poured into me, and full of what He had taught me of the nature of the All and of the loftiest Vision.

And I began to preach unto men the Beauty of Devotion and of Gnosis:

O ye people, earth-born folk, ye who have given yourselves to drunkenness and sleep and ignorance of God, be sober now, cease from your surfeit, cease to be glamoured by irrational sleep!

28. And when they heard, they came with one accord. Whereon I say:

Ye earth-born folk, why have ye given yourselves up to Death, while yet ye have the power of sharing Deathlessness? Repent,

O ye, who walk with Error arm in arm and make of Ignorance the sharer of your board; get ye out from the light of Darkness, and take your part in Deathlessness, forsake Destruction!

29. And some of them with jests upon their lips departed [from me], abandoning themselves unto the Way of Death; others entreated to be taught, casting themselves before my feet.

But I made them arise, and I became a leader of the Race towards home, teaching the words (logoi), how and in what way they shall be saved. I sowed in them the words (logoi) of wisdom; of Deathless Water were they given to drink.

And when even was come and all sun's beams began to set, I bade them all give thanks to God. And when they had brought to an end the giving of their thanks, each man returned to his own resting place.

30. But I recorded in my heart Man-Shepherd's benefaction, and with my every

hope fulfilled more than rejoiced. For body's sleep became the soul's awakening, and closing of the eyes - true vision, pregnant with Good my silence, and the utterance of my word (logos) begetting of good things.

All this befell me from my Mind, that is Man-Shepherd, Word (Logos) of all masterhood, by whom being God-inspired I came unto the Plain of Truth. Wherefore with all my soul and strength thanksgiving give I unto Father-God.

31. Holy art Thou, O God, the universals' Father.

Holy art Thou, O God, whose Will perfects itself by means of its own Powers.

Holy art Thou, O God, who willeth to be known and art known by Thine own.

Holy art Thou, who didst by Word (Logos) make to consist the things that are.

Holy art Thou, of whom All-nature hath been made an image.

Holy art Thou, whose Form Nature hath never made.

Holy art Thou, more powerful than all power.

Holy art Thou, transcending all pre-eminence.

Holy Thou art, Thou better than all praise.

Accept my reason's offerings pure, from soul and heart for aye stretched up to Thee, O Thou unutterable, unspeakable, Whose Name naught but the Silence can express.

32. Give ear to me who pray that I may never of Gnosis fail, [Gnosis] which is our common being's nature; and fill me with Thy Power, and with this Grace [of Thine], that I may give the Light to those in ignorance of the Race, my Brethren, and Thy Sons.

For this cause I believe, and I bear witness; I go to Life and Light. Blessed art Thou, O Father. Thy Man would holy be as Thou art holy, even as Thou gave him Thy full authority [to be].

CHAPTER TWO

To Asclepius

NOTES ON THE TEXT: This dialogue sets forth the difference between the physical and metaphysical worlds in the context of Greek natural philosophy. Some of the language is fairly technical: the "errant spheres" of sections 6 and 7 are the celestial spheres carrying the planets, while the "inerrant sphere" is that of the fixed stars. It is useful to

keep in mind, also, that "air" and "spirit" are interchangeable concepts in Greek thought, and that the concept of the Good has a range of implications which don't come across in the English word: one is that the good of any being, in Greek thought, was also that being's necessary goal.

1. **Hermes:** All that is moved, Asclepius, is it not moved in something and by something?

Asclepius: Assuredly.

H: And must not that in which it›s moved be greater than the moved?

A: It must.

H: Mover, again, has greater power than moved?

A: It has, of course.

H: The nature, furthermore, of that in which it›s moved must be quite other from the nature of the moved?

A: It must completely.

2. **H:** Is not, again, this cosmos vast,

[so vast] that than it there exists no body greater?

A: Assuredly.

H: And massive, too, for it is crammed with multitudes of other mighty frames, nay, rather all the other bodies that there are?

A: It is.

H: And yet the cosmos is a body?

A: It is a body.

H: And one that›s moved?

3. **A:** Assuredly.

H: Of what size, then, must be the space in which it›s moved, and of what kind [must be] the nature [of that space]? Must it not be far vaster [than the cosmos], in order that it may be able to find room for its continued course, so that the moved may not be cramped for want of room and lose its motion?

A: Something, Thrice-greatest one, it needs must be, immensely vast.

4. **H:** And of what nature? Must it not be, Asclepius, of just the contrary? And is not

contrary to body bodiless?

A: Agreed.

H: Space, then, is bodiless. But bodiless must either be some godlike thing or God [Himself]. And by «some godlike thing» I mean no more the generable [i.e., that which is generated] but the ingenerable.

5. If, then, space be some godlike thing, it is substantial; but if 'tis God [Himself], it transcends substance. But it is to be thought of otherwise [than God], and in this way.

God is first "thinkable" <or "intelligible"> for us, not for Himself, for that the thing that's thought doth fall beneath the thinker's sense. God then cannot be "thinkable" unto Himself, in that He's thought of by Himself as being nothing else but what He thinks. But he is "something else" for us, and so He's thought of by us.

6. If space is, therefore, to be thought, [it should] not, [then, be thought as] God, but space. If God is also to be thought, [He should] not [be conceived] as space, but as

energy that can contain [all space].

Further, all that is moved is moved not in the moved but in the stable. And that which moves [another] is of course stationary, for 'tis impossible that it should move with it.

A: How is it, then, that things down here, Thrice-greatest one, are moved with those that are [already] moved? For thou hast said the errant spheres were moved by the inerrant one.

H: This is not, O Asclepius, a moving with, but one against; they are not moved with one another, but one against the other. It is this contrariety which turneth the resistance of their motion into rest. For that resistance is the rest of motion.

7. Hence, too, the errant spheres, being moved contrarily to the inerrant one, are moved by one another by mutual contrariety, [and also] by the spable one through contrariety itself. And this can otherwise not be.

The Bears up there <i.e., Ursa Major and

Minor>, which neither set nor rise, think'st thou they rest or move?

A: They move, Thrice-greatest one.

H: And what their motion, my Asclepius?

A: Motion that turns for ever round the same.

H: But revolution - motion around same - is fixed by rest. For «round-the-same» doth stop «beyond-same». «Beyond-same» then, being stopped, if it be steadied in «round-same» - the contrary stands firm, being rendered ever stable by its contrariety.

8. Of this I'll give thee here on earth an instance, which the eye can see. Regard the animals down here - a man, for instance, swimming! The water moves, yet the resistance of his hands and feet give him stability, so that he is not borne along with it, nor sunk thereby.

A: Thou hast, Thrice-greatest one, adduced a most clear instance.

H: All motion, then, is caused in station and by station.

The motion, therefore, of the cosmos (and of every other hylic <i.e., material> animal) will not be caused by things exterior to the cosmos, but by things interior [outward] to the exterior - such [things] as soul, or spirit, or some such other thing incorporeal.

'Tis not the body that doth move the living thing in it; nay, not even the whole [body of the universe a lesser] body e'en though there be no life in it.

9. **A:** What meanest thou by this, Thrice-greatest one? Is it not bodies, then, that move the stock and stone and all the other things inanimate?

H: By no means, O Asclepius. The something-in-the-body, the that-which-moves the thing inanimate, this surely›s not a body, for that it moves the two of them - both body of the lifter and the lifted? So that a thing that›s lifeless will not move a lifeless thing. That which doth move [another thing] is animate, in that it is the mover.

Thou seest, then, how heavy laden is the

soul, for it alone doth lift two bodies. That things, moreover, moved are moved in something as well as moved by something is clear.

10. **A:** Yea, O Thrice-greatest one, things moved must needs be moved in something void.

H: Thou sayest well, O [my] Asclepius! For naught of things that are is void. Alone the «is-not» is void [and] stranger to subsistence. For that which is subsistent can never change to void.

A: Are there, then, O Thrice-greatest one, no such things as an empty cask, for instance, and an empty jar, a cup and vat, and other things like unto them?

H: Alack, Asclepius, for thy far-wandering from the truth! Think›st thou that things most full and most replete are void?

11. **A:** How meanest thou, Thrice-greatest one?

H: Is not air body?

A: It is.

H: And doth this body not pervade all things, and so, pervading, fill them? And «body»; doth body not consist from blending of the «four» <elements>? Full, then, of air are all thou callest void; and if of air, then of the «four».

Further, of this the converse follows, that all thou callest full are void - of air; for that they have their space filled out with other bodies, and, therefore, are not able to receive the air therein. These, then, which thou dost say are void, they should be hollow named, not void; for they not only are, but they are full of air and spirit.

12. **A:** Thy argument (logos), Thrice-greatest one, is not to be gainsaid; air is a body. Further, it is this body which doth pervade all things, and so, pervading, fill them. What are we, then, to call that space in which the all doth move?

H: The bodiless, Asclepius.

A: What, then, is Bodiless?

H: ‹Tis Mind and Reason (logos), whole

out of whole, all self-embracing, free from all body, from all error free, unsensible to body and untouchable, self stayed in self, containing all, preserving those that are, whose rays, to use a likeness, are Good, Truth, Light beyond light, the Archetype of soul.

A: What, then, is God?

13. **H:** Not any one of these is He; for He it is that causeth them to be, both all and each and every thing of all that are. Nor hath He left a thing beside that is-not; but they are all from things-that-are and not from things-that-are-not. For that the things-that-are-not have naturally no power of being anything, but naturally have the power of the inability-to-be. And, conversely, the things-that-are have not the nature of some time not-being.

14. **A:** What say'st thou ever, then, God is?

H: God, therefore, is not Mind, but Cause that the Mind is; God is not Spirit, but Cause that Spirit is; God is not Light, but Cause that the Light is. Hence one should honor God with these two names [the Good and Father] - names which pertain to Him alone and no one else.

For no one of the other so-called gods, no one of men, or daimones, can be in any measure Good, but God alone; and He is Good alone and nothing else. The rest of things are separable all from the Good's nature; for [all the rest] are soul and body, which have no place that can contain the Good.

15. For that as mighty is the Greatness of the Good as is the Being of all things that are - both bodies and things bodiless, things sensible and intelligible things. Call thou not, therefore, aught else Good, for thou would'st imious be; nor anything at all at any time call God but Good alone, for so thou would'st again be impious.

16. Though, then, the Good is spoken of by all, it is not understood by all, what thing

it is. Not only, then, is God not understood by all, but both unto the gods and some of the men they out of ignorance do give the name of Good, though they can never either be or become Good. For they are very different from God, while Good can never be distinguished from Him, for that God is the same as Good.

The rest of the immortal ones are nonetheless honored with the name of God, and spoken of as gods; but God is Good not out of courtesy but out of nature. For that God's nature and the Good is one; one os the kind of both, from which all other kinds [proceed].

The Good is he who gives all things and naught receives. God, then, doth give all things and receive naught. God, then, is Good, and Good is God.

17. The other name of God is Father, again because He is the that-which-maketh-all. The part of father is to make.

Wherefore child-making is a very great and

a most pious thing in life for them who think aright, and to leave life on earth without a child a very great misfortune and impiety; and he who hath no child is punished by the daimones after death.

And this is the punishment: that that man's soul who hath no child, shall be condemned unto a body with neither man's nor woman's nature, a thing accursed beneath the sun.

Wherefore, Asclepius, let not your sympathies be with the man who hath no child, but rather pity his mishap, knowing what punishment abides for him.

Let all that has been said then, be to thee, Asclepius, an introduction to the gnosis of the nature of all things.

CHAPTER THREE

The Sacred Sermon

NOTES ON THE TEXT: This brief (and possibly somewhat garbled) text recounts the creation and nature of the world in terms much like those of the Poemandres. The major theme is the renewal of all things in a cyclic universe, with the seven planetary rulers again playing a major role.

1. The Glory of all things is God, Godhead and Godly Nature. Source of the things that are is God, who is both Mind and Nature - yea Matter, the Wisdom that reveals all things. Source [too] is Godhead - yea Nature, Energy, Necessity, and End, and Making-new-again.

Darkness that knew no bounds was in Abyss, and Water [too] and subtle Breath intelligent; these were by Power of God in Chaos.

Then Holy Light arose; and there collected 'neath Dry Space <literally: "sand"> from out Moist Essence Elements; and all the Gods do separate things out from fecund Nature.

2. All things being undefined and yet unwrought, the light things were assigned unto the height, the heavy ones had their foundations laid down underneath the moist part of Dry Space, the universal things being bounded off by Fire and hanged in Breath to keep them up.

And Heaven was seen in seven circles; its

Gods were visible in forms of stars with all their signs; while Nature had her members made articulate together with the Gods in her. And [Heaven's] periphery revolved in cyclic course, borne on by Breath of God.

3. And every God by his own proper power brought forth what was appointed him. Thus there arose four-footed beasts, and creeping things, and those that in the water dwell, and things with wings, and everything that beareth seed, and grass, and shoot of every flower, all having in themselves seed of again-becoming.

And they selected out the births of men for gnosis of the works of God and attestation of the energy of Nature; the multitude of men for lordship over all beneath the heaven and gnosisofitsblessings, thattheymightincrease in increasing and multiply in multitude, and every soul infleshed by revolution of the Cyclic Gods, for observation of the marvels of Heaven and Heaven's Gods' revolution, and of the works of God and energy of

Nature, for tokens of its blessings, for gnosis of the power of God, that they might know the fates that follow good and evil [deeds] and learn the cunning work of all good arts.

4. [Thus] there begins their living and their growing wise, according to the fate appointed by the revolution of the Cyclic Gods, and their deceasing for this end.

And there shall be memorials mighty of their handiworks upon the earth, leaving dim trace behind when cycles are renewed.

For every birth of flesh ensouled, and of the fruit of seed, and every handiwork, though it decay, shall of necessity renew itself, both by the renovation of the Gods and by the turning-round of Nature's rhythmic wheel.

For that whereas the Godhead is Nature's ever-making-new-again the cosmic mixture, Nature herself is also co-established in that Godhead.

CHAPTER FOUR

The Cup or Monad

NOTES ON THE TEXT: This short text gives an unusually lucid overview of the foundations of Hermetic thought. The stress on rejection of the body and its pleasures, and on the division of humanity into those with Mind and those without, are reminiscent of some of the so-called "Gnostic" writings of the same period. The idea that the division

is a matter of choice, on the other hand, is a pleasant variation on the almost Calvinist flavor of writings such as the Apocalypse of Adam.

Mead speculates that the imagery of the Cup in this text may have a distant connection, by way of unorthodox ideas about Communion, with the legends of the Holy Grail.

1. Hermes: With Reason (Logos), not with hands, did the World-maker make the universal World; so that thou shouldst think of him as everywhere and ever-being, the Author of all things, and One and Only, who by His Will all beings hath created.

This Body of Him is a thing no man can touch, or see, or measure, a body inextensible, like to no other frame. 'Tis neither Fire nor Water, Air nor Breath; yet all of them come from it. Now being Good he willed to consecrate this [Body] to Himself alone, and set its Earth in order and adorn it.

2. So down [to Earth] He sent the Cosmos of this Frame Divine - man, a life that cannot die, and yet a life that dies. And o'er [all other] lives and over Cosmos [too], did man excel by reason of the Reason (Logos) and the Mind. For contemplator of God's works did man become; he marvelled and did strive to know their Author.

3. Reason (Logos) indeed, O Tat, among all men hath He distributed, but Mind not yet; not that He grudgeth any, for grudging cometh not from Him, but hath its place below, within the souls of men who have no Mind.

Tat: Why then did God, O father, not on all bestow a share of Mind?

H: He willed, my son, to have it set up in the midst for souls, just as it were a prize.

4. T: And where hath He set it up?

H: He filled a mighty Cup with it, and sent it down, joining a Herald [to it], to whom He gave command to make this proclamation to the hearts of men:

Baptize thyself with this Cup's baptism, what heart can do so, thou that hast faith thou canst ascend to him that hath sent down the Cup, thou that dost know for what thoudidst come into being!

As many then as understood the Herald's tidings and doused themselves in Mind, became partakers in the Gnosis; and when they had "received the Mind" they were made "perfect men".

But they who do not understand the tidings, these, since they possess the aid of Reason [only] and not Mind, are ignorant wherefor they have come into being and whereby.

5. The senses of such men are like irrational creatures'; and as their [whole] make-up is in their feelings and their impulses, they fail in all appreciation of <lit.: "they do not wonder at"> those things which really are worth contemplation. These center all their thought upon the pleasures of the body and its appetites, in the belief that for its

sake man hath come into being.

But they who have received some portion of God's gift, these, Tat, if we judge by their deeds, have from Death's bonds won their release; for they embrace in their own Mind all things, things on the earth, things in the heaven, and things above the heaven - if there be aught. And having raised themselves so far they sight the Good; and having sighted it, they look upon their sojourn here as a mischance; and in disdain of all, both things in body and the bodiless, they speed their way unto that One and Only One.

6. This is, O Tat, the Gnosis of the Mind, Vision of things Divine; God-knowledge is it, for the Cup is God's.

T: Father, I, too, would be baptized.

H: Unless thou first shall hate thy Body, son, thou canst not love thy Self. But if thou lov'st thy Self thou shalt have Mind, and having Mind thou shalt share in the Gnosis.

T: Father, what dost thou mean?

H: It is not possible, my son, to give thyself to both - I mean to things that perish and to things divine. For seeing that existing things are twain, Body and Bodiless, in which the perishing and the divine are understood, the man who hath the will to choose is left the choice of one or the other; for it can never be the twain should meet. And in those souls to whom the choice is left, the waning of the one causes the other's growth to show itself.

7. Now the choosing of the Better not only proves a lot most fair for him who makes the choice, seeing it makes the man a God, but also shows his piety to God. Whereas the [choosing] of the Worse, although it doth destroy the "man", it doth only disturb God's harmony to this extent, that as processions pass by in the middle of the way, without being able to do anything but take the road from others, so do such men move in procession through the world led by their bodies' pleasures.

8. This being so, O Tat, what comes from God hath been and will be ours; but that which is dependent on ourselves, let this press onward and have no delay, for 'tis not God, 'tis we who are the cause of evil things, preferring them to good.

Thou see'st, son, how many are the bodies through which we have to pass, how many are the choirs of daimones, how vast the system of the star-courses [through which our Path doth lie], to hasten to the One and Only God.

For to the Good there is no other shore; It hath no bounds; It is without an end; and for Itself It is without beginning, too, though unto us it seemeth to have one - the Gnosis.

9. Therefore to It Gnosis is no beginning; rather is it [that Gnosis doth afford] to us the first beginning of its being known.

Let us lay hold, therefore, of the beginning. and quickly speed through all [we have to pass].

`Tis very hard, to leave the things we

have grown used to, which meet our gaze on every side, and turn ourselves back to the Old Old [Path].

Appearances delight us, whereas things which appear not make their believing hard.

Now evils are the more apparent things, whereas the Good can never show Itself unto the eyes, for It hath neither form nor figure.

Therefore the Good is like Itself alone, and unlike all things else; or 'tis impossible that That which hath no body should make Itself apparent to a body.

10. The "Like's" superiority to the "Unlike" and the "Unlike's" inferiority unto the "Like" consists in this:

The Oneness being Source and Root of all, is in all things as Root and Source. Without [this] Source is naught; whereas the Source [Itself] is from naught but itself, since it is Source of all the rest. It is Itself Its Source, since It may have no other Source.

The Oneness then being Source,

containeth every number, but is contained by none; engendereth every number, but is engendered by no other one.

11. Now all that is engendered is imperfect, it is divisible, to increase subject and to decrease; but with the Perfect [One] none of these things doth hold. Now that which is increasable increases from the Oneness, but succumbs through its own feebleness when it no longer can contain the One.

And now, O Tat, God's Image hath been sketched for thee, as far as it can be; and if thou wilt attentively dwell on it and observe it with thine heart's eyes, believe me, son, thou'lt find the Path that leads above; nay, that Image shall become thy Guide itself, because the Sight [Divine] hath this peculiar [charm], it holdeth fast and draweth unto it those who succeed in opening their eyes, just as, they say, the magnet [draweth] iron.

CHAPTER FIVE

Though Unmanifest God is Most Manifest

1. I WILL RECOUNT to thee this sermon (logos) too, O Tat, that thou may'st cease to be without the mysteries of the God beyond all name. And mark thou well how that which to the many seems unmanifest, will grow most manifest for thee.

Now were it manifest, it would not be.

For all that is made manifest is subject to becoming, for it hath been made manifest. But the Unmanifest for ever is, for It doth not desire to be made manifest. It ever is, and maketh manifest all other things.

Being Himself unmanifest, as ever being and ever making-manifest, Himself is not made manifest. God is not made Himself; by thinking-manifest <i.e., thinking into manifestation>, He thinketh all things manifest.

Now "thinking-manifest" deals with things made alone, for thinking-manifest is nothing else than making.

2. He, then, alone who is not made, 'tis clear, is both beyond all power of thinking-manifest, and is unmanifest.

And as He thinketh all things manifest, He manifests through all things and in all, and most of all in whatsoever things He wills to manifest.

Do thou, then, Tat, my son, pray first unto our Lord and Father, the One-and-Only

One, from whom the One doth come, to show His mercy unto thee, in order that thou mayest have the power to catch a thought of this so mighty God, one single beam of Him to shine into thy thinking. For thought alone "sees" the Unmanifest, in that it is itself unmanifest.

If, then, thou hast the power, He will, Tat, manifest to thy mind's eyes. The Lord begrudgeth not Himself to anything, but manifests Himself through the whole world.

Thou hast the power of taking thought, of seeing it and grasping it in thy own "hands", and gazing face to face upon God's Image. But if what is within thee even is unmanifest to thee, how, then, shall He Himself who is within thy self be manifest for thee by means of [outer] eyes?

3. But if thou wouldst "see" him, bethink thee of the sun, bethink thee of moon's course, bethink thee of the order of the stars. Who is the One who watcheth o'er that order? For every order hath its boundaries

marked out by place and number.

The sun's the greatest god of gods in heaven; to whom all of the heavenly gods give place as unto king and master. And he, this so-great one, he greater than the earth and sea, endures to have above him circling smaller stars than him. Out of respect to Whom, or out of fear of Whom, my son, [doth he do this]?

Nor like nor equal is the course each of these stars describes in heaven. Who [then] is He who marketh out the manner of their course and its extent?

4. The Bear up there that turneth round itself, and carries round the whole cosmos with it - Who is the owner of this instrument? Who He who hath set round the sea its bounds? Who He who hath set on its seat the earth?

For, Tat, there is someone who is the Maker and the Lord of all these things. It cound not be that number, place and measure could be kept without someone to make them. No order whatsoever could be made by that which lacketh place and lacketh measure; nay, even this is not without a lord, my son. For if the orderless lacks something, in that it is not lord of order's path, it also is beneath a lord - the one who hath not yet ordained it order.

5. Would that it were possible for thee to get thee wings, and soar into the air, and, poised midway 'tween earth and heaven, behold the earth's solidity, the sea's fluidity (the flowings of its streams), the spaciousness of air, fire's swiftness, [and] the coursing of the stars, the swiftness of heaven's circuit round them [all]!

Most blessed sight were it, my son, to see all these beneath one sway - the motionless in motion, and the unmanifest made manifest; whereby is made this order of the cosmos and the cosmos which we see of order.

6. If thou would'st see Him too through things that suffer death, both on the earth and

in the deep, think of a man's being fashioned in the womb, my son, and strictly scrutinize the art of Him who fashions him, and learn who fashioneth this fair and godly image of the Man.

Who [then] is He who traceth out the circles of the eyes; who He who boreth out the nostrils and the ears; who He who openeth [the portal of] the mouth; who He who doth stretch out and tie the nerves; who He who channels out the veins; who He who hardeneth the bones; who He who covereth the flesh with skin; who He who separates the fingers and the joints; who He who widens out a treading for the feet; who He who diggeth out the ducts; who He who spreadeth out the spleen; who he who shapeth heart like to a pyramid; who He who setteth ribs together; who He who wideneth the liver out; who He who maketh lungs like to a sponge; who He who maketh belly stretch so much; who he who doth make prominent the parts most honorable, so that they may be seen, while hiding out of sight those of least honor?

7. Behold how many arts [employed] on one material, how many labors on one single sketch; and all exceeding fair, and all in perfect measure, yet all diversified! Who made them all? What mother, or what sire, save God alone, unmanifest, who hath made all things by His Will?

8. And no one saith a statue or a picture comes to be without a sculptor or [without] a painter; doth [then] such workmanship as this exist without a Worker? What depth of blindness, what deep impiety, what depth of ignorance! See, [then] thou ne'er, son Tat, deprivest works of Worker!

Nay, rather is He greater than all names, so great is He, the Father of them all. For verily He is the Only One, and this is His work, to be a father.

9. So, if thou forcest me somewhat too bold, to speak, His being is conceiving of all things and making [them].

And as without its maker its is impossible that anything should be, so ever is He not unless He ever makes all things, in heaven, in air, in earth, in deep, in all of cosmos, in every part that is and that is not of everything. For there is naught in all the world that is not He.

He is Himself, both things that are and things that are not. The things that are He hath made manifest, He keepeth things that are not in Himself.

10. He is the God beyond all name; He the unmanifest, He the most manifest; He whom the mind [alone] can contemplate, He visible to the eyes [as well]; He is the one of no body, the one of many bodies, nay, rather He of every body.

Naught is there which he is not. For all are He and He is all. And for this cause hath He all names, in that they are one Father's. And for this cause hath He Himself no nome, in that He's Father of [them] all.

Who, then, may sing Thee praise of Thee,

or [praise] to Thee?

Whither, again, am I to turn my eyes to sing Thy praise; above, below, within, without?

There is no way, no place [is there] about Thee, nor any other thing of things that are.

All [are] in Thee; all [are] from Thee, O Thou who givest all and takest naught, for Thou hast all and naught is there Thou hast not.

11. And when, O Father, shall I hymn Thee? For none can seize Thy hour or time.

For what, again, shall I sing hymn? For things that Thou hast made, or things Thou hast not? For things Thou hast made manifest, or things Thou hast concealed?

How, further, shall I hymn Thee? As being of myself? As having something of mine own? As being other?

For that Thou art whatever I may be; Thou art whatever I may do; Thou art whatever I may speak.

For Thou art all, and there is nothing else which Thou art not. Thou art all that which doth exist, and Thou art what doth not exist -

Mind when Thou thinkest, and Father when Thou makest, and God when Thou dost energize, and Good and Maker of all things.

For that the subtler part of matter is the air, of air the soul, of soul the mind, and of mind God.

CHAPTER SIX

In God Alone is Good and Elsewhere Nowhere

NOTES ON THE TEXT: This sermon on the nature of the Good, like To Asclepius **(CH II), relies on the technical language of classical Greek philosophy - a point which some of Mead's translations tend to obscure. "The Good," in Greek thought, is also the self-caused and**

self-sufficient, and thus has little in common with later conceptions of "goodness," just as the Latin word virtus and the modern Christian concept of "virtue" are very nearly opposites despite their etymological connection. The word "passion" here also needs to be understood in its older sense, as the opposite of "action" (cf. "active" and "passive").

The negative attitude toward humanity and the cosmos which appears in this text contrasts sharply with the more positive assessment found, for example, in the Poemandres (CH I) or in the Asclepius - a reminder that these documents are relics of a diverse and not necessarily consistent school of thought

1. Good, O Asclepius, is in none else save in God alone; nay, rather, Good is God Himself eternally.

If it be so, [Good] must be essence, from every kind of motion and becoming free (though naught is free from It), possessed of stable energy around Itself, never too little, nor too much, an ever-full supply. [Though] one, yet [is It] source of all; for what supplieth all is Good. When I, moreover, say [supplieth] altogether [all], it is for ever Good. But this belongs to no one else save God alone.

For He stands not in need of any thing, so that desiring it He should be bad; nor can a single thing of things that are be lost to him, on losing which He should be pained; for pain is part of bad.

Nor is there aught superior to Him, that He should be subdued by it; nor any peer to Him to do Him wrong, or [so that] He should fall in love on its account; nor aught that gives no ear to Him, whereat He should grow angry; nor wiser aught, for Him to envy.

2. Now as all these are non-existent in His being, what is there left but Good alone?

For just as naught of bad is to be found in such transcendent Being, so too in no one of the rest will Good be found.

For in them are all of the other things <i.e., those things which are not Good> - both in the little and the great, both in each severally and in this living one that's greater than them all and the mightiest [of them] <i.e., the cosmos>.

For things subject to birth abound in passions, birth in itself being passible. But where there's passion, nowhere is there Good; and where is Good, nowhere a single passion. For where is day, nowhere is night; and where is night, day is nowhere.

Wherefore in genesis the Good can never be, but only be in the ingenerate.

But seeing that the sharing in all things hath been bestowed on matter, so doth it share in Good.

In this way is the Cosmos Good; that, in so far as it doth make all things, as far as making goes it's Good, but in all other things it is not Good. For it's both passible and subject unto motion, and maker of things passible.

3. Whereas in man by greater or less of bad is good determined. For what is not too bad down here, is good, and good down here is the least part of bad.

It cannot, therefore, be that good down here should be quite clean of bad, for down here good is fouled with bad; and being fouled, it stays no longer good, and staying not it changes into bad.

In God alone, is, therefore, Good, or rather Good is God Himself.

So then, Asclepius, the name alone of Good is found in men, the thing itself nowhere [in them], for this can never be.

For no material body doth contain It - a thing bound on all sides by bad, by labors, pains, desires and passions, by error and by foolish thoughts.

And greatest ill of all, Asclepius, is that each of these things that have been said above, is thought down here to be the greatest good.

And what is still an even greater ill, is belly-lust, the error that doth lead the band of all the other ills - the thing that makes us turn down here from Good.

4. And I, for my part, give thanks to God, that He hath cast it in my mind about the Gnosis of the Good, that it can never be It should be in the world. For that the world is "fullness" of the bad, but God of Good, and Good of God.

The excellencies of the Beautiful are round the very essence [of the Good]; nay, they do seem too pure, too unalloyed; perchance 'tis they that are themselves Its essences.

For one may dare to say, Asclepius - if essence, sooth, He have - God's essence is the Beautiful; the Beautiful is further also Good.

There is no Good that can be got from objects in the world. For all the things that fall beneath the eye are image-things and pictures as it were; while those that do not meet [the eye are the realities], especially the [essence] of the Beautiful and Good.

Just as the eye cannot see God, so can it not behold the Beautiful and Good. For that they are integral parts of God, wedded to Him alone, inseparate familiars, most beloved, with whom God is Himself in love, or they with God.

5. If thou canst God conceive, thou shalt conceive the Beautiful and Good, transcending Light, made lighter than the Light by God. That Beauty is beyond compare, inimitate that Good, e'en as God is Himself.

As, then, thou dost conceive of God, conceive the Beautiful and Good. For they cannot be joined with aught of other things that live, since they can never be divorced from God.

Seek'st thou for God, thou seekest for the Beautiful. One is the Path that leadeth unto It - Devotion joined with Gnosis.

6. And thus it is that they who do not know

and do not tread Devotion's Path, do dare to call man beautiful and good, though he have ne'er e'en in his visions seen a whit that's Good, but is enveloped with every kind of bad, and thinks the bad is good, and thus doth make unceasing use of it, and even feareth that it should be ta'en from him, so straining every nerve not only to preserve but even to increase it.

Such are the things that men call good and beautiful, Asclepius - things which we cannot flee or hate; for hardest thing of all is that we've need of them and cannot live without them.

CHAPTER SEVEN

The Greatest Ill Among Men is Ignorance of God

1. WHITHER STUMBLE YE, sots, who have sopped up the wine of ignorance and can so far not carry it that ye already even spew it forth?

Stay ye, be sober, gaze upwards with the [true] eyes of the heart! And if ye cannot all, yet ye at least who can!

For that the ill of ignorance doth pour o`er all the earth and overwhelm the soul that's battened down within the body, preventing it from fetching port within Salvation's harbors.

2. Be ye then not carried off by the fierce flood, but using the shore-current <lit., "back-current" or "up-current">, ye who can, make for Salvation's port, and, harboring there, seek ye for one to take you by the hand and lead you unto Gnosis' gates.

Where shines clear Light, of every darkness clean; where not a single soul is drunk, but sober all they gaze with their hearts' eyes on Him who willeth to be seen.

No ear can hear Him, nor can eye see Him, nor tongue speak of Him, but [only] mind and heart.

But first thou must tear off from thee the cloak which thou dost wear - the web of ignorance, the ground of bad, corruption's chain, the carapace of darkness, the living death, sensation's corpse, the tomb thou carriest with thee, the robber in thy house, who through the things he loveth, hateth thee, and through the things he hateth, bears thee malice.

3. Such is the hateful cloak thou wearest - that throttles thee [and holds thee] down to it, in order that thou may'st not gaze above, and having seen the Beauty of the Truth, and Good that dwells therein, detest the bad of it; having found out the plot that it hath schemed against thee, by making void of sense those seeming things which men think senses.

For that it hath with mass of matter blocked them up and crammed them full of loathsome lust, so that thou may'st not hear about the things that thou should'st hear, nor see the things thou should'st see.

CHAPTER EIGHT

That No One of Existing Things Doth Perish

NOTES ON THE TEXT: The idea of cyclic change central to CH III, "The Sacred Sermon", also takes center stage here. A current of ancient speculation grounded in astrology held that as the planets returned after vast cycles of time to the same positions, so all events on earth

would repeat themselves precisely into eternity in the future - and had done so from eternity in the past. The technical term for this recurrence, apocatastasis, is the word Mead translates as "restoration" in the beginning of section 4.

Mead footnotes this tractate as "obscure" and "faulty" in places, and his translation of the beginning of section 3 is conjectural.

1. [Hermes:] Concerning Soul and Body, son, we now must speak; in what way Soul is deathless, and whence comes the activity in composing and dissolving Body.

For there's no death for aught of things [that are]; the thought this word conveys, is either void of fact, or [simply] by the knocking off a syllable what is called "death", doth stand for "deathless".

For death is of destruction, and nothing in the Cosmos is destroyed. For if Cosmos is second God, a life <or living creature>

that cannot die, it cannot be that any part of this immortal life should die. All things in Cosmos are parts of Cosmos, and most of all is man, the rational animal.

2. For truly first of all, eternal and transcending birth, is God the universals' Maker. Second is he "after His image", Cosmos, brought into being by Him, sustained and fed by Him, made deathless, as by his own Sire, living for aye, as ever free from death.

Now that which ever-liveth, differs from the Eternal; for He hath not been brought to being by another, and even if He have been brought to being, He hath not been brought to being by Himself, but ever is brought into being.

For the Eternal, in that It is eternal, is the all. The Father is Himself eternal of Himself, but Cosmos hath become eternal and immortal by the Father.

3. And of the matter stored beneath it <i.e., beneath the cosmos>, the Father made of

it a universal body, and packing it together made it spherical - wrapping it round the life - [a sphere] which is immortal in itself, and that doth make materiality eternal.

But He, the Father, full-filled with His ideas, did sow the lives <or living creatures> into the sphere, and shut them in as in a cave, willing to order forth the life with every kind of living.

So He with deathlessness enclosed the universal body, that matter might not wish to separate itself from body's composition, and so dissolve into its own [original] unorder.

For matter, son, when it was yet incorporate <i.e., not yet formed into bodies>, was in unorder. And it doth still retain down here this [nature of unorder] enveloping the rest of the small lives <or living creatures> - that increase-and-decrease which men call death.

4. It is round earthly lives that this unorder doth exist. For that the bodies of the heavenly ones preserve one order allotted

to them by the Father as their rule; and it is by the restoration of each one [of them] this order is preserved indissolute.

The "restoration" of bodies on the earth is thus their composition, whereas their dissolution restores them to those bodies which can never be dissolved, that is to say, which know no death. Privation, thus, of sense is brought about, not loss of bodies.

5. Now the third life - Man, after the image of the Cosmos made, [and] having mind, after the Father's will, beyond all earthly lives - not only doth have feeling with the second God <i.e., the Cosmos>, but also hath conception of the first; for of the one 'tis sensible as of a body, while of the other it conceives as bodiless and the Good Mind.

Tat: Doth then this life not perish?

Hermes: Hush, son! and understand what God, what Cosmos [is], what is a life that cannot die, and what a life subject to dissolution.

Yea, understand the Cosmos is by God and in God; but Man by Cosmos and in Cosmos.

The source and limit and the constitution of all things is God.

CHAPTER NINE

On Thought and Sense

NOTES ON THE TEXT: This somewhat diffuse essay covers a series of topics, starting with (and to some extent from) the concept that the set of perceptions we call "thoughts" and the set we call "sensory perceptions" are not significantly different from each other. The implications of this idea play a significant role in later Hermetic thought, particularly in the areas of magic and the Art of Memory; in this tractate, though, the issues involved are barely touched, and the argument wanders into moral dualisms and the equally important, but distinct, idea that the Cosmos is itself a divine creative power.

Section 10, in which understanding is held up as the source and precondition of belief, should probably be seen as part of the same ancient debate on the roles of faith and reason that gave rise to Tertullian's famous credo quia absurdum ("I believe because it is absurd").

1. I gave the Perfect Sermon (Logos) yesterday, Asclepius; today I think it right, as sequel thereunto, to go through point by point the Sermon about Sense.

Now sense and thought do seem to differ, in that the former has to do with matter, the latter has to do with substance. But unto

me both seem to be at-one and not to differ
- in men I mean. In other lives <or living
creatures> sense is at-oned with Nature, but
in men thought.

Now mind doth differ just as much from
thought as God doth from divinity. For that
divinity by God doth come to be, and by
mind thought, the sister of the word (logos)
and instruments of one another. For neither
doth the word (logos) find utterance without
thought, nor is thought manifested without
word.

2. So sense and thought both flow together
into man, as though they were entwined with
one another. For neither without sensing
can one think, nor without thinking sense.

But it is possible [they say] to think a thing
apart from sense, as those who fancy sights
in dreams. But unto me it seems that both
of these activities occur in dream-sight, and
sense doth pass out of the sleeping to the
waking state.

For man is separated into soul and body,

and only when the two sides of his sense agree together, does utterance of its thought conceived by mind take place.

3. For it is mind that doth conceive all thoughts - good thoughts when it receives the seeds from God, their contraries when [it receiveth them] from the daimonials; no part of Cosmos being free of daimon, who stealthily doth creep into the daimon who's illumined by God's light <i.e., the human soul>, and sow in him the seed of its own energy.

And mind conceives the seed thus sown, adultery, murder, parricide, [and] sacrilege, impiety, [and] strangling, casting down precipices, and all such other deeds as are the work of evil daimons.

4. The seeds of God, 'tis true, are few, but vast and fair, and good - virtue and self-control, devotion. Devotion is God-gnosis; and he who knoweth God, being filled with all good things, thinks godly thoughts and not thoughts like the many [think].

For this cause they who Gnostic are, please not the many, nor the many them. They are thought mad and laughted at; they're hated and despised, and sometimes even put to death.

For we did say that bad must needs dwell on earth, where 'tis in its own place. Its place is earth, and not Cosmos, as some will sometimes say with impious tongue.

But he who is a devotee of God, will bear with all - once he has sensed the Gnosis. For such an one all things, e'en though they be for others bad, are for him good; deliberately he doth refer them all unto the Gnosis. And, thing most marvelous, 'tis he alone who maketh bad things good.

5. But I return once more to the Discourse (Logos) on Sense. That sense doth share with thought in man, doth constitute him man. But 'tis not [every] man, as I have said, who benefits by thought; for this man is material, that other one substantial.

For the material man, as I have said,

[consorting] with the bad, doth have his seed of thought from daimons; while the substantial men [consorting] with the Good, are saved by God.

Now God is Maker of all things, and in His making, He maketh all [at last] like to Himself; but they, while they're becoming good by exercise of their activity, are unproductive things.

It is the working of the Cosmic Course that maketh their becomings what they are, befouling some of them with bad and others of them making clean with good.

For Cosmos, too, Asclepius, possesseth sense-and-thought peculiar to itself, not like that of man; 'tis not so manifold, but as it were a better and a simpler one.

6. The single sense-and-thought of Cosmos is to make all things, and make them back into itself again, as Organ of the Will of God, so organized that it, receiving all the seeds into itself from God, and keeping them within itself, may make all manifest,

and [then] dissolving them, make them all new again; and thus, like a Good Gardener of Life, things that have been dissolved, it taketh to itself, and giveth them renewal once again.

There is no thing to which it gives not life; but taking all unto itself it makes them live, and is at the same time the Place of Life and its Creator.

7. Now bodies matter [-made] are in diversity. Some are of earth, of water some, some are of air, and some of fire.

But they are all composed; some are more [composite], and some are simpler. The heavier ones are more [composed], the lighter less so.

It is the speed of Cosmos' Course that works the manifoldness of the kinds of births. For being a most swift Breath, it doth bestow their qualities on bodies together with the One Pleroma - that of Life.

8. God, then, is Sire of Cosmos; Cosmos, of all in Cosmos. And Cosmos is God's Son;

but things in Cosmos are by Cosmos.

And properly hath it been called Cosmos [Order]; for that it orders all with their diversity of birth, with its not leaving aught without its life, with the unweariedness of its activity, the speed of its necessity, the composition of its elements, and order of its creatures.

The same, then, of necessity and propriety should have the name of Order.

The sense-and-thought, then, of all lives doth come into them from without, inbreathed by what contains [them all]; whereas Cosmos receives them once for all together with its coming into being, and keeps them as a gift from God.

9. But God is not, as some suppose, beyond the reach of sense-and-thought. It is through superstition men thus impiously speak.

For all the things that are, Asclepius, all are in God, are brought by God to be, and do depend on Him - both things that act through bodies, and things that through soul-substance make [other things] to move, and things that make things live by means of spirit, and things that take unto themselves the things that are worn out.

And rightly so; nay, I would rather say, He doth not have these things; but I speak forth the truth, He is them all Himself. He doth not get them from without, but gives them out [from Him].

This is God's sense-and-thought, ever to move all things. And never time shall be when e'en a whit of things that are shall cease; and when I say "a whit of things that are", I mean a whit of God. For thigs that are, God hath; nor aught [is there] without Him, nor [is] He without aught.

10. These things should seem to thee, Asclepius, if thou dost understand them, true; but if thou dost not understand, things not to be believed.

To understand is to believe, to not believe is not to understand.

My word (logos) doth go before [thee] to the truth. But mighty is the mind, and when it hath been led by word up to a certain point, it hath the power to come before [thee] to the truth.

And having thought o'er all these things, and found them consonant with those which have already been translated by the reason, it hath [e'en now] believed, and found its rest in that Fair Faith.

To those, then, who by God['s good aid] do understand the things that have been said [by us] above, they're credible; but unto those who understand them not, incredible.

Let so much, then, suffice on thought-and-sense.

CHAPTER TEN

The Key

NOTES: THIS LONGER TRACTATE presents itself explicitly as a summary or abridgement of the General Sermons (CH II-IX), and discusses the Hermetic view of knowledge and its role in the lives and afterlives of human beings. The attentive reader will notice certain contradictions between the afterlife-teachings of this and previous tractates.

One of the central concepts of The Key, and of Hermetic thought generally, is the distinction between ordinary discursive knowledge which can be expressed in words (in Greek, episteme, which Mead translates somewhat clumsily as "science") and transcendent, unitive knowledge which cannot be communicated (in Greek, gnosis, which Mead simply and sensibly leaves untranslated). The same distinction can be found in many systems of mystical thought. Unlike most of these, though, the Hermetic teachings place value on both.

Readers without much experience in the jargon of Classical philosophy will want to remember that "hylic" means "material", "passible" means "subject to outside forces or to suffering", and "intelligible" means "belonging to the realm of the Mind", and "motion" includes all kinds of change. The special

implications of "good" in Greek thought - of self-sufficiency and desirability - should also be kept in mind.

The delightful irony of the Zen moment early in section 9, when Hermes - in the middle of this very substantial lecture - defines the good and pious man as "he who doth not say much or lend his ear to much" and thus rules out both himself and his audience, seems to have been lost on subsequent commentators.

1. Hermes: My yesterday's discourse (logos) I did devote to thee, Asclepius, and so 'tis [only] right I should devote toafy's to Tat; and this the more because 'tis the abridgement of the General Sermons (Logoi) which he has had addressed to him.

"God, Father and the Good", then, Tat, hath the same nature, or more exactly, energy.

For nature is a predicate of growth, and used of things that change, both mobile and immobile, that is to say, both human and divine, each one of which He willeth into being.

But energy consists in something else, as we have shown in treating of the rest, both things divine and human things; which thing we ought to have in mind when treating of the Good.

2. God's energy is then His Will; further His essence is to will the being of all things. For what is "God and Father and the Good" but the "to be" of all that are not yet? Nay, subsistence self of everything that is; this, then, is God, this Father, this the Good; to Him is added naught of all the rest.

And though the Cosmos, that is to say the Sun, is also sire himself to them that share in him; yet so far is he not the cause of good unto the lives, he is not even of their living.

So that e'en if he be a sire, he is entirely so by compulsion of the Good's Good-will, apart from which nor being nor becoming could e'er be.

3. Again, the parent is the children's cause,

both on the father's and the mother's side, only by sharing in the Good's desire [that doth pour] through the Sun. It is the Good which doeth the creating.

And such a power can be possessed by no one else than Him alone who taketh naught, but wills all things to be; I will not, Tat, say "makes".

For that the maker is defective for long periods (in which he sometimes makes, and sometimes doth not make) both in the quality and in the quantity [of what he makes]; in that he sometimes maketh them so many and such like, and sometimes the reverse.

But "God and Father and the Good" is [cause] for all to be. So are at least these things for those who can see.

4. For It doth will to be, and It is both Itself and most of all by reason of Itself. Indeed, all other things beside are just bacause of It; for the distinctive feature of the Good is "that it should be known". Such is the Good, O Tat.

Tat: Thou hast, O father, filled us so full of this so good and fairest sight, that thereby my mind's eye hath now become for me almost a thing to worship.

For that the vision of the Good doth not, like the sun's beam, firelike blaze on the eyes and make them close; nay, on the contrary, it shineth forth and maketh to increase the seeing of the eye, as far as e'er a man hath the capacity to hold the inflow of the radiance that the mind alone can see.

Not only does it come more swiftly down to us, but it does us no harm, and is instinct with all immortal life.

5. They who are able to drink in a somewhat more than others of this Sight, ofttimes from out the body fall asleep in this fairest Spectacle, as was the case with Uranus and Cronus, our forebears. may this be out lot too, O father mine!

Hermes: Yea, may it be, my son! But as it is, we are not yet strung to the Vision, and not as yet have we the power our mind's eye to unfold and gaze upon the Beauty of the Good - Beauty that naught can e'er corrupt or any comprehend.

For only then wilt thou upon It gaze when thou canst say no word concerning It. For Gnosis of the Good is holy silence and a giving holiday to every sense.

6. For neither can he who perceiveth It, perceive aught else; nor he who gazeth on It, gaze on aught else; nor hear aught else, nor stir his body any way. Staying his body's every sense and every motion he stayeth still.

And shining then all round his mond, It shines through his whole soul, and draws it out of body, transforming all of him to essence.

For it is possible, my son, that a man's soul should be made like to God, e'en while it still is in a body, if it doth contemplate the Beauty of the Good.

7. Tat: Made like to God? What dost thou,

father, mean?

Hermes: Of every soul apart are transformations, son.

Tat: What meanest thou? Apart?

Hermes: Didst thou not, in the General Sermons, hear that from one Soul - the All-soul - come all these souls which are made to revolve in all the cosmos, as though divided off?

Of these souls, then, it is that there are many changes, some to a happier lot and some to [just] the contrary of this.

Thus some that were creeping things change into things that in the water dwell, the souls of water things change to earth-dwellers, those that live on earth change to things with wings, and souls that live in air change to men, while human souls reach the first step of deathlessness changed into daimones.

And so they circle to the choir of the Inerrant Gods; for of the Gods there are two choirs, the one Inerrant, and the other Errant. And this is the most perfect glory of the soul.

8. But if a soul on entering the body of a man persisteth in its vice, it neither tasteth deathlessness nor shareth in the Good; but speeding back again it turns into the path that leads to creeping things. This is the sentence of the vicious soul.

And the soul's vice is ignorance. For that the soul who hath no knowledge of the things that are, or knowledge of their nature, or of Good, is blinded by the body's passions and tossed about.

This wretched soul, not knowing what she is, becomes the slave of bodies of strange form in sorry plight, bearing the body as a load; not as the ruler, but the ruled. This [ignorance] is the soul's vice.

9. But on the other hand the virtue of the soul is Gnosis. For he who knows, he good and pious is, and still while on the earth divine.

Tat: But who is such an one, O father mine?

Hermes: He who doth not say much or

lend his ear to much. For he who spendeth time in arguing and hearing arguments, doth shadow-fight. For "God, the Father and the Good", is not to be obtained by speech or hearing.

And yet though this is so, there are in all the beings senses, in that they cannot without senses be.

But Gnosis is far different from sense. For sense is brought about by that which hath the mastery o'er us, while Gnosis is the end <i.e., goal> of science, and science is God's gift.

10. All science is incorporeal, the instrument it uses being the mind, just as the mind employs the body.

Both then come into bodies, [I mean] both things that are cognizable by mond alone and things material. For all things must consist out of antithesis and contrariety; and this can otherwise not be.

Tat: Who then is this material God of whom thou speakest?

Hermes: Cosmos is beautiful, but is not good - for that it is material and freely passible; and though it is the first of all things passible, yet is it in the second rank of being and wanting in itself.

And though it never hath itself its birth in time, but ever is, yet is its being in becoming, becoming for all time the genesis of qualities and quantities; for it is mobile and all material motion's genesis.

11. It is intelligible rest that moves material motion in this way, since Cosmos is a sphere - that is to say, a head. And naught of head above's material, as naught of feet below's intelligible, but all material.

And head itself is moved in a sphere-like way - that is to say, as head should move, is mind.

All then that are united to the "tissue" of this "head" (in which is soul) are in their nature free from death - just as when body hath been made in soul, are things that hath more soul than body.

Whereas those things which are at greater distance from this "tissue" - there, where are things which have a greater share of body than of soul - are by their nature subject unto death.

The whole, however, is a life; so that the universe consists of both the hylic and of the intelligible.

12. Again, the Cosmos is the first of living things, while man is second after it, though first of things subject to death.

Man hath the same ensouling power in him as all the rest of living things; yet is he not only not good, but even evil, for that he's subject unto death.

For though the Cosmos also is not good in that it suffers motion, it is not evil, in that it is not subject to death. But man, in that he's subject both to motion and to death, is evil.

13. Now then the principles of man are this-wise vehicled: mind in the reason (logos), the reason in the soul, soul in the spirit <or, rather, vital spirits>, and spirit in the body.

Spirit pervading [body] by means of veins and arteries and blood, bestows upon the living creature motion, and as it were doth bear it in a way.

For this cause some do think the soul is blood, in that they do mistake its nature, not knowing that [at death] it is iteh spirit that must first withdraw into the soul, whereon the blood congeals and veins and arteries are emptied, and then the living creature <or life> is withdrawn; and this is body's death.

14. Now from one Source all things depend; while Source [dependeth] from the One and Only [One]. Source is, moreover, moved to become Source again; whereas the One standeth perpetually and is not moved.

Three then are they: "God, the Father and the Good", Cosmos and man.

God doth contain Cosmos; Cosmos [containeth] man. Cosmos is e'er God's Son, man as it were Cosmos' child.

15. Not that, however, God ignoreth man;

nay, right well doth He know him, and willeth to be known.

This is the sole salvation for a man - God's Gnosis. This is the Way Up to the Mount.

By Him alone the soul becometh good, not whiles is good, whiles evil, but [good] out of necessity.

Tat: What dost thou mean, Thrice-greatest one?

Hermes: Behold an infant's soul, my son, that is not yet cut off, because its body is still small and not as yet come unto its full bulk.

Tat: How?

Hermes: A thing of beauty altogether is [such a soul] to see, not yet befouled by body's passions, still all but hanging from the Cosmic Soul!

But when the body grows in bulk and draweth down the soul into its mass, then doth the soul cut off itself and bring upon itself forgetfulness, and no more shareth in the Beautiful and the Good. And this forgetfulness becometh vice.

16. It is the same for them who go out from the body.

For when the soul withdraws into itself, the spirit doth contract itself within the blood, and the soul within the spirit. And then the mind, stripped of its wrappings, and naturally divine, taking unto itself a fiery body, doth traverse every space, after abandoning the soul unto its judgement and whatever chastisement it hath deserved.

Tat: What dost thou, father, mean by this? The mind is parted from soul and soul from spirit? Whereas thou said'st the soul was the mind's vesture, and the soul's the spirit.

17. Hermes: The hearer, son, should think with him who speaks and breathe with him; nay, he should have a hearing subtler than the voice of him who speaks.

It is, son, in a body made of earth that this arrangement of the vestures comes to pass. For in a body made of earth it is impossible the mind should take its seat itself by its own self in nakedness.

For neither is it possible on the one hand the earthly body should contain so much immortality, nor on the other that so great a virtue should endure a body passible in such close contact with it. It taketh, then, the soul for as it were an envelope.

And soul itself, being too and thing divine, doth use the spirit as its envelope, while spirit doth pervade the living creature.

18. When then the mind doth free itself from the earth-body, it straightway putteth on its proper robe of fire, with which it could not dwell in an earth-body.

For earth doth not bear fire; for it is all set in a blaze even by a small spark. And for this cause is water poured around earth, to be a guard and wall, to keep the blazing of the fire away.

But mind, the swiftest thing of all divine outthinkings, and swifter than all elements, hath for its body fire.

For mind being builder doth use the fire as tool for the construction of all things - the

Mind of all [for the construction] of all things, but that of man only for things on earth.

Stript of its fire the mind on earth cannot make things divine, for it is human in its dispensation.

19. The soul in man, however - not every soul, but one that pious is - is a daimonic something and divine.

And such a soul when from the body freed, if it have fought the fight of piety - the fight of piety is to know God and to do wrong to no man - such a soul becomes entirely mind.

Whereas the impious soul remains in its own essence, chastised by its own self, and seeking for an earthly body where to enter, if only it be human.

For that no other body can contain a human soul; nor is it right that any human soul should fall into the body of a thing that doth possess no reason. For that the law of God is this: to guard the human soul from such tremendous outrage.

20. Tat: How father, then, is a man's soul

chastised?

Hermes: What greater chastisement of any human soul can there be, son, than lack of piety? What fire has so fierce a flame as lack of piety? What ravenous beast so mauls the body as lack of piety the very soul?

Dost thou not see what hosts of ills the impious soul doth bear?

It shrieks and screams: I burn; I am ablaze; I know not what to cry or do; ah, wretched me, I am devoured by all the ills that compass me about; alack, poor me, I neither see nor hear!

Such are the cries wrung from a soul chastised; not, as the many think, and thou, son, dost suppose, that a [man's] soul, passing from body, is changed into a beast.

Such is a very grave mistake, for that the way a soul doth suffer chastisement is this:

21. When mind becomes a daimon, the law requires that it should take a fiery body to execute the services of God; and entering

in the soul most impious it scourgeth it with whips made of its sins.

And then the impious soul, scourged with its sins, is plunged in murders, outrage, blasphemy, in violence of all kinds, and all the other things whereby mankind is wronged.

But on the pious soul the mind doth mount and guide it to the Gnosis' Light. And such a soul doth never tire in songs of praise [to God] and pouring blessing on all men, and doing good in word and deed to all, in imitation of its Sire.

22. Wherefore, my son, thou shouldst give praise to God and pray that thou mayst have thy mind Good Mind. It is, then, to a better state the soul doth pass; it cannot to a worse.

Further there is an intercourse of souls; those of the gods have intercourse with those of men, and those of men with souls of creatures which possess no reason.

The higher, further, have in charge the

lower; the gods look after men, men after animals irrational, while God hath charge of all; for He is higher than them all and all are less than He.

Cosmos is subject, then, to God, man to the Cosmos, and irrationals to man. But God is o'er them all, and God contains them all.

God's rays, to use a figure, are His energies; the Cosmos's are natures, the arts and sciences are man's.

The energies act through the Cosmos, thence through the nature-rays of Cosmos upon man; the nature-rays [act] through the elements, man [acteth] through the sciences and arts.

23. This is the dispensation of the universe, depending from the nature of the One, pervading [all things] through the Mind, than which is naught diviner nor of greater energy; and naught a greater means for the at-oning men to gods and gods to men.

He, [Mind,] is the Good Daimon. Blessed the soul that is most filled with Him, and wretched is the soul that's empty of the Mind.

Tat: Father, what dost thou mean, again?

Hermes: Dost think then, son, that every soul hath the Good [Mind]? For 'tis of Him we speak, not of the mind in service of which we were just speaking, the mind sent down for [the soul's] chastisement.

24. For soul without the mind "can neither speak nor act". For oftentimes the mind doth leave the soul, and at that time the soul neither sees nor understands, but is just like a thing that hath no reason. Such is the power of mind.

Yet doth it not endure a sluggish soul, but leaveth such a soul tied to the body and bound tight down by it. Such soul, my son, doth not have Mind; and therefore such an one should not be called a man. For that man is a thing-of-life <or animal> divine; man is not measured with the rest of lives of things upon the earth, but with the lives above in heaven, who are called gods.

Nay more, if we must boldly speak the truth,

the true "man" is e'en higher than the gods, or at the [very] least the gods and men are very whit in power each with the other equal.

25. For no one of the gods in heaven shall come down to the earth, o'er-stepping heaven's limit; whereas man doth mount up to heaven and measure it; he knows what things of it are high, what things are low, and learns precisely all things else besides. And greater thing than all; without e'en quitting earth, he doth ascend above. So vast a sweep doth he possess of ecstasy.

For this cause can a man dare say that man on earth is god subject to death, while god in heaven is man from death immune.

Wherefore the dispensation of all things is brought about by means of there, the twain - Cosmos and Man - but by the One.

CHAPTER ELEVEN

Mind unto Hermes

NOTES ON THE TEXT: This complex text is written as a revelation from the divine Mind - the "Man-Shepherd" of CH I - to Hermes, concerning the nature of God and the universe. Difficult enough in its own right, it has been made more so by some of Mead's prose. I have tried to insert clarifications where these are most needed.

Some notes on terminology may also be useful. The term Aeon here, as in many of the so-called "Gnostic" writings, refers to the timeless and spaceless realm of ideal being. The word cosmos means both "order" and "beauty" - the same root appears in the word "cosmetic". Additionally, the words genesis and becoming in the translation are the same word in the Greek original.

Finally, the word "inactive" in square brackets near the beginning of section 13 is Mead's, intended to fill a lacuna in the text. The more usual conjecture, as he comments, is "apart from God"

1. Mind: Master this sermon (logos), then, Thrice-greatest Hermes, and bear in mind the spoken words; and as it hath come unto Me to speak, I will no more delay.

Hermes: As many men say many things, and these diverse, about the All and Good, I have not learned the truth. Make it, then, clear to me, O Master mine! For I can trust the explanation of these things, which comes from Thee alone.

2. Mind: Hear [then], My son, how standeth God and All.

God; Aeon; Cosmos; Time; Becoming.

God maketh Aeon; Aeon, Cosmos; Cosmos, Time; and Time, Becoming <or Genesis>.

The Good - the Beautiful, Wisdom, Blessedness - is <the> essence, as it were, of God; of Aeon, <the essence is> Sameness; of Cosmos, Order; of Time, Change; and of Becoming, Life and Death.

The energies of God are Mind and Soul; of Aeon, lastingness and deathlessness; of Cosmos, restoration and the opposite thereof; of Time, increase and decrease; and of Becoming, quality.

Aeon is, then, in God; Cosmos, in Aeon; in Cosmos; Time; in Time, Becoming.

Aeon stands firm round God; Cosmos is moved in Aeon; Time hath its limits <or is accomplished> in the Cosmos; Becoming doth become in Time.

3. The source, therfore, of all is God; their essence, Aeon; their matter, Cosmos.

God's power is Aeon; Aeon's work is Cosmos - which never hath become, yet ever doth become by Aeon.

Therefore will Cosmos never be destroyed, for Aeon's indestructible; nor doth a whit of things in Cosmos perish, for Cosmos is enwrapped by Aeon round on every side.

Hermes: But God's Wisdom - what is that?

Mind: The Good and Beautiful, and Blessedness, and Virtue's all, and Aeon.

Aeon, then, ordereth [Cosmos], imparting deathlessness and lastingness to matter.

4. For its beginning doth depend on Aeon, as Aeon doth on God.

Now Genesis <or Becoming> and Time, in Heaven and upon the Earth, are of two natures.

In Heaven they are unchangeable and indestructible, but on the Earth they're subject unto change and to destruction.

Further, the Aeon's soul is God; the Cosmos' soul is Aeon; the Earth's soul, Heaven.

And God <is> in Mind; and Mind, in Soul; and Soul, in Matter; and all of them through Aeon.

But all this Body, in which are all the bodies, is full of Soul; and Soul is full of Mind, and Mind of God.

It <i.e., Soul> fills it <i.e., the Body of the Cosmos> from within, and from without encircles it, making the All to live.

Without, this vast and perfect Life [encircles] Cosmos; within, it fills [it with] all lives; above, in Heaven, continuing in sameness; below, on Earth, changing becoming.

5. And Aeon doth preserve this [Cosmos], or by Necessity, or by Foreknowledge, or by Nature, or by whatever else a man supposes or shall suppose. And all is this - God energizing.

The Energy of God is Power that naught can e'er surpass, a Power with which no one can make comparison of any human thing at all, or any thing divine.

Wherefore, O Hermes, never think that aught of things above or things below is like to God, for thou wilt fall from truth. For naught is like to That which hath no like, and is Alone and One.

And do not ever think that any other can possibly possess His power; for what apart from Him is there of life, and deathlessness and change of quality? For what else should He make?

God's not inactive, since all things [then] would lack activity; for all are full of God.

But neither in the Cosmos anywhere, nor in aught else, is there inaction. For that "inaction" is a name that cannot be applied to either what doth make or what is made.

6. But all things must be made; both ever made, and also in accordance with the influence of every space.

For He who makes, is in them all; not stablished in some one of them, nor making one thing only, but making all.

For being Power, He energizeth in the things He makes and is not independent of them - although the things He makes are subject to Him.

Now gaze through Me upon the Cosmos that's now subject to thy sight; regard its Beauty carefully - Body in pure perfection, though one than which there's no more ancient one, ever in prime of life, and ever-young, nay, rather, in even fuller and yet fuller prime!

7. Behold, again, the seven subject Worlds; ordered by Aeon's order, and with their varied course full-filling Aeon!

[See how] all things [are] full of light, and nowhere [is there] fire; for 'tis the love and the blending of the contraries and the dissimilars that doth give birth to light down shining by the energy of God, the Father of all good, the Leader of all order, and Ruler of the seven world-orderings!

[Behold] the Moon, forerunner of them all,

the instrument of nature, and the transmuter of its lower matter!

[Look at] the Earth set in the midst of All, foundation of the Cosmos Beautiful, feeder and nurse of things on Earth!

And contemplate the multitude of deathless lives, how great it is, and that of lives subject to death; and midway, between both, immortal [lives] and mortal, [see thou] the circling Moon.

8. And all are full of soul, and all are moved by it, each in its proper way; some round the Heaven, others around the Earth; [see] how the right [move] not unto the left, nor yet the left unto the right; nor the above below, nor the below above.

And that all there are subject unto Genesis, My dearest Hermes, thou hast no longer need to learn of Me. For that they bodies are, have souls, and they are moved.

But 'tis impossible for them to come together into one without some one to bring them [all] together. It must, then, be that such a one as this must be some one who's wholly One.

9. For as the many motions of them [all] are different, and as their bodies are not like, yet has one speed been ordered for them all, it is impossible that there should be two or more makers for them.

For that one single order is not kept among "the many"; but rivalry will follow of the weaker with the stronger, and they will strive.

And if the maker of the lives that suffer change and death, should be another <from the maker of the immortals>, he would desire to make the deathless ones as well; just as the maker of the deathless ones, [to make the lives] that suffer death.

But come! if there be two - if matter's one, and Soul is one, in whose hands would there be the distribution for the making? Again, if both of them have some of it, in whose hands may be the greater part?

10. But thus conceive it, then; that every living body doth consist of soul and matter,

whether [that body be] of an immortal, or a mortal, or an irrational [life].

For that all living bodies are ensouled; whereas, upon the other hand, those that live not, are matter by itself.

And, in like fashion, Soul when in its self is, after its own maker, cause of life; but the cause of all life is He who makes the things that cannot die.

Hermes: How, then, is it that, first, lives subject to death are other than the deathless ones? And, next, how is it that Life which knows no death, and maketh deathlessness, doth not make animals immortal?

11. Mind: First, that there is some one who does these things, is clear; and, next, that He is also One, is very manifest. For, also, Soul is one, and Life is one, and Matter one.

Hermes: But who is He?

Mind: Who may it other be than the One God? Whom else should it beseem to put Soul into lives but God alone? One, then, is God.

It would indeed be most ridiculous, if when thou dost confess the Cosmos to be one, Sun one, Moon one, and Godhead one, thou shouldst wish God Himself to be some one or other of a number!

12. All things, therefore, He makes, in many [ways]. And what great thing is it for God to make life, soul, and deathlessness, and change, when thou [thyself] dost do so many things?

For thou dost see, and speak, and hear, and smell, and taste, and touch, and walk, and think, and breathe. And it is not one man who smells, another one who walks, another one who thinks, and [yet] another one who breathes. But one is he who doth all these.

And yet no one of these could be apart from God. For just as, should thou cease from these, thou wouldst no longer be a living thing, so also, should God cease from them (a thing not law to say), no longer is He God.

13. For if it hath been shown that no thing

can [inactive] be, how much less God? For if there's aught he doth not make (if it be law to say), He is imperfect. But if He is not only not inactive, but perfect [God], then He doth make all things.

Give thou thyself to Me, My Hermes, for a little while, and thou shalt understand more easily how that God's work is one, in order that all things may be - that are being made, or once have been, or that are going to be made. And this is, My beloved, Life; this is the Beautiful; this is the Good; this, God.

14. And if thou wouldst in practice understand [this work], behold what taketh place with thee desiring to beget. Yet this is not like unto that, for He doth not enjoy.

For that indeed He hath no other one to share in what He works, for working by Himself, He ever is at work, Himself being what He doth. For did He separate Himself from it, all things would [then] collapse, and all must die, Life ceasing.

But if all things are lives, and also Life is one; then, one is God. And, furthermore, if all are lives, both those in Heaven and those on Earth, and One Life in them all is made to be by God, and God is it <i.e., God is the One Life> - then, all are made by God.

Life is the making-one of Mind and Soul; accordingly Death is not the destruction of those that are at-oned, but the dissolving of their union.

15. Aeon, moreover, is God's image; Cosmos [is] Aeon's; the Sun, of Cosmos; and Man, [the image] of the Sun.

The people call change death, because the body is dissolved, and life, when it's dissolved, withdraws to the unmanifest. But in this sermon (logos), Hermes, My beloved, as thou dost hear, I say the Cosmos also suffers change - for that a part of it each day is made to be in the unmanifest - yet it is ne'er dissolved.

These are the passions of the Cosmos - revolvings and concealments; revolving is conversion and concealment renovation.

16. The Cosmos is all-formed - not having forms external to itself, but changing them itself within itself. Since, then, Cosmos is made to be all-formed, what may its maker be? For that, on the one hand, He should not be void of all form; and, on the other hand, if He's all-formed, He will be like the Cosmos. Whereas, again, has He a single form, He will thereby be less than Cosmos.

What, then, say we He is? - that we may not bring round our sermon (logos) into doubt; for naught that mind conceives of God is doubtful.

He, then, hath one idea, which is His own alone, which doth not fall beneath the sight, being bodiless, and [yet] by means of bodies manifesteth all [ideas]. And marvel not that there's a bodiless idea.

17. For it is like the form of reason (logos) and mountain-tops in pictures. For they appear to stand out strongly from the rest, but really are quite smooth and flat.

And now consider what is said more boldly, but more truly!

Just as man cannot live apart from Life, so neither can God live without [His] doing good. For this is as it were the life and motion as it were of God - to move all things and make them live.

18. Now some of the things said should bear a sense peculiar to themselves. So understand, for instance, what I'm going to say.

All are in God, [but] not as lying in a place. For place is both a body and immovable, and things that lie do not have motion.

Now things lie one way in the bodiless, another way in being made manifest.

Think, [then,] of Him who doth contain them all; and think, that than the bodiless naught is more comprehensive, or swifter, or more potent, but it is the most comprehensive, the swiftest, and most potent of them all.

19. And, thus, think from thyself, and bid thy soul go unto any land, and there more quickly

than thy bidding will it be. And bid it journey oceanwards; and there, again, immediately 'twill be, not as if passing on from place to place, but as if being there.

And bid it also mount to heaven; and it will need no wings, not will aught hinder it, nor fire of sun, nor auther, nor vortex-swirl, nor bodies of the other stars; but, cutting through them all, it will soar up to the last Body [of them all]. And shouldst thou will to break through this as well, and contemplate what is beyond - if there be aught beyond the Cosmos; it is permitted thee.

20. Behold what power, what swiftness, thou dost have! And canst thou do all of these things, and God not [do them]?

Then, in this way know God; as having all things in Himself as thoughts, the whole Cosmos itself.

If, then, thou dost not make thyself like unto God, thou canst not know Him. For like is knowable unto like [alone].

Make, [then,] thyself to grow to the same

stature as the Greatness which transcends all measure; leap forth from every body; transcend all time; become Eternity <literally, Aeon>; and [thus] shalt thou know God.

Conceiving nothing is impossible unto thyself, think thyself deathless and able to know all - all arts, all sciences, the way of every life.

Become more lofty than all height, and lower than all depth. Collect into thyself all senses of [all] creatures - of fire, [and] water, dry and moist. Think that thou art at the same time in every place - in earth, in sea, in sky; not yet begotten, in the womb, young, old, [and] dead, in after-death conditions.

And if thou knowest all these things at once - times, places, doings, qualities, and quantities; thou canst know God.

21. But if thou lockest up thy soul within thy body, and dost debase it, saying: I nothing know; I nothing can; I fear the sea; I cannot scale the sky; I know not who I was, who I shall be - what is there [then] between [thy]

God and thee?

For thou canst know naught of things beautiful and good so long as thou dost love thy body and art bad.

The greatest bad there is, is not to know God's Good; but to be able to know [Good], and will, and hope, is a Straight Way, the Good's own [Path], both leading there and easy.

If thou but settest thy foot thereon, 'twill meet thee everywhere, 'twill everywhere be seen, both where and when thou dost expect it not - waking, sleeping, sailing, journeying, by night, by day, speaking, [and] saying naught. For there is naught that is not image of the Good.

22. Hermes: Is God unseen?

Mind: Hush! Who is more manifest than He? For this one reason hath He made all things, that through them all thou mayest see Him.

This is the Good of God, this [is] His Virtue - that He may be manifest through all.

For naught's unseen, even of things that are without a body. Mind sees itself in thinking, God in making.

So far these things have been made manifest to thee, Thrice-greatest one! Reflect on all the rest in the same way with thyself, and thou shalt not be led astray.

CHAPTER TWELVE

About the Common Mind

NOTES ON THE TEXT: The "common mind" discussed in this dialogue is the same Mind which appears as a divine power in other parts of the Hermetic literature. It is identical, as well, with the "Good Daimon" whose words are quoted at several points here and elsewhere.

The Greek word logos - which means both "word" and "reason", among other

things-is central to much of the argument, and it's unfortunate that English has no way to express the same complex of meanings. The praise of reason in parts 13-14 is also, and equally, a praise of human language, and this sort of double meaning plays a part elsewhere in this and other parts of the Hermetic literature.

1. Hermes: The Mind, O Tat, is of God's very essence - (if such a thing as essence of God there be) - and what that is, it and it only knows precisely.

The Mind, then, is not separated off from God's essentiality, but is united to it, as light to sun.

This Mind in men is God, and for this cause some of mankind are gods, and their humanity is nigh unto divinity.

For the Good Daimon said: "Gods are immortal men, and men are mortal gods."

2. But in irrational lives Mind is their nature. For where is Soul, there too is Mind; just as

where Life, there is there also Soul.

But in irrational lives their soul is life devoid of mind; for Mind is the in-worker of the souls of men for good - He works on them for their own good.

In lives irrational He doth co-operate with each one's nature; but in the souls of men He counteracteth them.

For every soul, when it becomes embodied, is instantly depraved by pleasure and by pain.

For in a compound body, just like juices, pain and pleasure seethe, and into them the soul, on entering in, is plunged.

3. O'er whatsoever souls the Mind doth, then, preside, to these it showeth its own light, by acting counter to their prepossessions, just as a good physician doth upon the body prepossessed by sickness, pain inflict, burning or lancing it for sake of health.

In just the selfsame way the Mind inflicteth pain on the soul, to rescue it from pleasure, whence comes its every ill.

The great ill of the soul is godlessness; then followeth fancy for all evil things and nothing good.

So, then, Mind counteracting it doth work good on the soul, as the physician health upon the body.

4. But whatsoever human souls have not the Mind as pilot, they share in the same fate as souls of lives irrational.

For [Mind] becomes co-worker with them, giving full play to the desires toward which [such souls] are borne - [desires] that from the rush of lust strain after the irrational; [so that such human souls,] just like irrational animals, cease not irrationally to rage and lust, nor are they ever satiate of ills.

For passions and irrational desires are ills exceeding great; and over these God hath set up the Mind to play the part of judge and executioner.

5. Tat: In that case, father mine, the teaching (logos) as to Fate, which previously thou didst explain to me, risks to be overset.

For that if it be absolutely fated for a man to fornicate, or commit sacrilege, or do some other evil deed, why is he punished - when he hath done the deed from Fate's necessity?

Hermes: All works, my son, are Fate's; and without Fate naught of things corporal - or <i.e., either> good, or ill - can come to pass.

But it is fated, too, that he who doeth ill, shall suffer. And for this cause he doth it - that he may suffer what he suffereth, because he did it.

6. But for the moment, [Tat,] let be the teaching as to vice and Fate, for we have spoken of these things in other [of our sermons]; but now our teaching (logos) is about the Mind: - what Mind can do, and how it is [so] different - in men being such and such, and in irrational lives [so] changed; and [then] again that in irrational lives it is not of a beneficial nature, while that in men it quencheth out the wrathful and the lustful elements.

Of men, again, we must class some as led by reason, and others as unreasoning.

7. But all men are subject to Fate, and genesis and change, for these are the beginning and the end of Fate.

And though all men do suffer fated things, those led by reason (those whom we said Mind doth guide) do not endure <a> like suffering with the rest; but, since they've freed themselves from viciousness, not being bad, they do not suffer bad.

Tat: How meanest thou again, my father? Is not the fornicator bad; the murderer bad; and [so with] all the rest?

Hermes: [I meant not that;] but that the Mind-led man, my son, though not a fornicator, will suffer just as though he had committed fornication, and though he be no murderer, as though he had committed murder.

The quality of change he can no more escape than that of genesis.

But it is possible for one who hath the

Mind, to free himself from vice.

8. Wherefore I've ever heard, my son, Good Daimon also say - (and had He set it down in written words, He would have greatly helped the race of men; for He alone, my son, doth truly, as the Firstborn God, gazing on all things, give voice to words (logoi) divine) - yea, once I heard Him say:

"All things are one, and most of all the bodies which the mind alone perceives. Our life is owing to [God's] Energy and Power and Aeon. His Mind is good, so is His Soul as well. And this being so, intelligible things know naught of separation. So, then, Mind, being Ruler of all things, and being Soul of God, can do whate'er it wills."

9. So do thou understand, and carry back this word (logos) unto the question thou didst ask before - I mean about Mind's Fate.

For if thou dost with accuracy, son, eliminate [all] captious arguments (logoi), thou wilt discover that of very truth the Mind, the Soul of God, doth rule o'er all - o'er Fate, and Law, and all things else; and nothing is impossible to it - neither o'er Fate to set a human soul, nor under Fate to set [a soul] neglectful of what comes to pass. Let this so far suffice from the Good Daimon's most good [words].

Tat: Yea, [words] divinely spoken, father mine, truly and helpfully. But further still explain me this.

10. Thou said'st that Mind in lives irrational worked in them as [their] nature, co-working with their impulses.

But impulses of lives irrational, as I do think, are passions.

Now if the Mind co-worketh with [these] impulses, and if the impulses of [lives] irrational be passions, then is Mind also passion, taking its color from the passions.

Hermes: Well put, my son! Thou questionest right nobly, and it is just that I as well should answer [nobly].

11. All things incorporeal when in a body are subject unto passion, and in the proper sense they are [themselves] all passions.

For every thing that moves itself is incorporeal; while every thing that's moved is body.

Incorporeals are further moved by Mind, and movement's <i.e., movement is> passion.

Both, then, are subject unto passion - both mover and the moved, the former being ruler and the latter ruled.

But when a man hath freed himself from body, then is he also freed from passion.

But, more precisely, son, naught is impassible, but all are passible.

Yet passion differeth from possibility; for that the one is active, while the other's passive.

Incorporeals moreover act upon themselves, for either they are motionless or they are moved; but whichsoe'er it be, it's passion.

But bodies are invaribly acted on, and therefore they are passible.

Do not, then, let terms trouble thee; action

and passion are both the selfsame thing. To use the fairer sounding term, however, does no harm.

12. Tat: Most clearly hast thou, father mine, set forth the teaching (logos).

Hermes: Consider this as well, my son; that these two things God hath bestowed on man beyond all mortal lives - both mind and speech (logos) equal to immortality. He hath the mind for knowing God and uttered speech (logos) for eulogy of Him.

And if one useth these for what he ought, he'll differ not a whit from the immortals. Nay, rather, on departing from the body, he will be guided by the twain unto the Choir of Gods and Blessed Ones.

13. Tat: Why, father mine! - do not the other lives make use of speech (logos)?

Hermes: Nay, son; but <i.e., only> use of voice; speech is far different from voice. For speech is general among all men, while voice doth differ in each class of living thing.

Tat: But with men also, father mine,

according to each race, speech differs.

Hermes: Yea, son, but man is one; so also speech is one and is interpreted, and it is found the same in Egypt, and in Persia, and in Greece.

Thou seemest, son, to be in ignorance of Reason's (Logos) worth and greatness. For that the Blessed God, Good Daimon, hath declared:

"Soul is in Body, Mind in Soul; but Reason (Logos) is in Mind, and Mind in God; and God is Father of [all] these."

14. The Reason, then, is the Mind's image, and Mind God's [image]; while Body is [the image] of the Form; and Form [the image] of the Soul.

The subtlest part of Matter is, then, Air <or vital spirit>; of Air, Soul; of Soul, Mind; and of Mind, God.

And God surroundeth all and permeateth all; while Mind Surroundeth Soul, Soul Air, Air Matter.

Necessity and Providence and Nature

are instruments of Cosmos and of Matter's ordering; while of intelligible things each is Essence, and Sameness is their Essence.

But of the bodies of the Cosmos each is many; for through possessiong Sameness, [these] composed bodies, though they do change from one into another of themselves, do natheless keep the incorruption of their Sameness.

15. Whereas in all the rest of composed bodies, of each there is a certain number; for without number structure cannot be, or composition, or decomposition.

Now it is units that give birth to number and increase it, and, being decomposed, are taken back again into themselves.

Matter is one; and this whole Cosmos - the mighty God and image of the mightier One, both with Him unified, and the conserver of the Will and Order of the Father - is filled full of Life.

Naught is there in it throughout the whole of Aeon, the Father's [everlasting] Reestablishment - nor of the whole, nor of the parts - which doth not live.

For not a single thing that's dead, hath been, or is, or shall be in [this] Cosmos.

For that the Father willed it should have Life as long as it should be. Wherefore it needs must be a God.

16. How then, O son, could there be in the God, the image of the Father, in the plenitude of Life - dead things?

For that death is corruption, and corruption destruction.

How then could any part of that which knoweth no corruption be corrupted, or any whit of him the God destroyed?

Tat: Do they not, then, my father, die - the lives in it, that are its parts?

Hermes: Hush, son! - led into error by the term in use for what takes place.

They do not die, my son, but are dissolved as compound bodies.

Now dissolution is not death, but dissolution of a compound; it is dissolved not so that it may be destroyed, but that it may become renewed.

For what is the activity of life? Is it not motion? What then in Cosmos is there that hath no motion? Naught is there, son!

17. Tat: Doth not Earth even, father, seem to thee to have no motion?

Hermes: Nay, son; but rather that she is the only thing which, though in very rapid motion, is also stable.

For how would it not be a thing to laugh at, that the Nurse of all should have no motion, when she engenders and brings forth all things?

For 'tis impossible that without motion one who doth engender, should do so.

That thou should ask if the fourth part <or element> is not inert, is most ridiculous; for the body which doth have no motion, gives sign of nothing but inertia.

18. Know, therefore, generally, my son, that all that is in Cosmos is being moved for increase or for decrease.

Now that which is kept moving, also lives; but there is no necessity that that which lives, should be all same.

For being simultaneous, the Cosmos, as a whole, is not subject to change, my son, but all its parts are subject unto it; yet naught [of it] is subject to corruption, or destroyed.

It is the terms employed that confuse men. For 'tis not genesis that constituteth life, but 'tis sensation; it is not change that constituteth death, but 'tis forgetfulness.

Since, then, these things are so, they are immortal all - Matter, [and] Life, [and] Spirit, Mind [and] Soul, of which whatever liveth, is composed.

19. Whatever then doth live, oweth its immortality unto the Mind, and most of all doth man, he who is both recipient of God, and co-essential with Him.

For with this life alone doth God consort; by visions in the night, by tokens in the day, and by all things doth He foretell the future unto him - by birds, by inward parts, by wind, by tree.

Wherefore doth man lay claim to know things past, things present and to come.

20. Observe this too, my son; that each one of the other lives inhabiteth one portion of the Cosmos - aquatic creatures water, terrene earth, and aery creatures air; while man doth use all these - earth, water air [and] fire; he seeth Heaven, too, and doth contact it with [his] sense.

But God surroundeth all, and permeateth all, for He is energy and power; and it is nothing difficult, my son, to conceive God.

21. But if thou wouldst Him also contemplate, behold the ordering of the Cosmos, and [see] the orderly behavior of its ordering <this is a play on the word "cosmos", which means "order, arrangement">; behold thou the Necessity of things made manifest, and [see] the Providence of things become and things becoming; behold how Matter is all-full of Life; [behold] this so great God in movement, with all the good and noble

[ones] - gods, daimones and men!

Tat: But these are purely energies, O father mine!

Hermes: If, then, they're purely energies, my son - by whom, then, are they energized except by God?

Or art thou ignorant, that just as Heaven, Earth, Water, Air, are parts of Cosmos, in just the selfsame way God's parts are Life and Immortality, [and] Energy, and Spirit, and Necessity, and Providence, and Nature, Soul, and Mind, and the Duration <that is, Aeon or Eternity> of all these that is called Good?

And there are naught of things that have become, or are becoming, in which God is not.

22. Tat: Is He in Matter, father, then?

Hermes: Matter, my son, is separate from God, in order that thou may'st attribute to it the quality of space. But what thing else than mass think'st thou it is, if it's not energized? Whereas if it be energized, by whom is it made so? For energies, we said, are parts of God.

By whom are, then, all lives enlivened? By whom are things immortal made immortal? By whom changed things made changeable?

And whether thou dost speak of Matter, of Body, or of Essence, know that these too are energies of God; and that materiality is Matter's energy, that corporeality is Bodies' energy, and that essentiality doth constituteth the energy of Essence; and this is God - the All.

23. And in the All is naught that is not God. Wherefore nor <i.e., neither> size, nor space, nor quality, nor form, nor time, surroundeth God; for He is All, and All surroundeth all, and permeateth all.

Unto this Reason (Logos), son, thy adoration and thy worship pay. There is one way alone to worship God; [it is] not to be bad.

CHAPTER THIRTEEN

The Secret Sermon on the Mountain

NOTES ON THE TEXT: This dialogue is in many ways the culmination of the whole Corpus, summing up the theory of the Hermetic system at the same time as it provides an intriguing glimpse at the practice. The focus of the dialogue is the experience of Rebirth, which involves

the replacement of twelve Tormentors within the self by ten divine Powers, leading to the awakening of knowledge of the self and God.

The "Secret Hymnody" (sections 17-20) is presented as a litany for worship, to be performed twice each day, at sunrise and sunset. It's interesting to note that while the sunrise worship is performed facing east, the sunset worship is done to the south; Egyptian tradition from Pharaonic times onward saw the west as the direction of death.

The usual difficulties with the multiple meanings of the Greek word logos appear in the translation, compounded by Mead's awkward style. Additionally, one of Mead's few evasions can be found in section 12, where he relates the twelve Tormentors to the "twelve types-of-life". This should more simply, and more accurately, have been translated as "the twelve signs of the Zodiac". The

Theosophical distaste for astrology may well have been involved here.

1. Tat: [Now] in the General Sermons, father, thou didst speak in riddles most unclear, conversing on Divinity; and when thou saidst no man could e'er be saved before Rebirth, thy meaning thou didst hide.

Further, when I became thy Suppliant, in Wending up the Mount, after thou hadst conversed with me, and when I longed to learn the Sermon (Logos) on Rebirth (for this beyond all other things is just the thing I know not), thou saidst, that thou wouldst give it me - "when thou shalt have become a stranger to the world".

Wherefore I got me ready and made the thought in me a stranger to the world-illusion.

And now do thou fill up the things that fall short in me with what thou saidst would give me the tradition of Rebirth, setting it forth in speech or in the secret way.

I know not, O Thrice-greatest one, from out what matter and what womb Man comes to birth, or of what seed.

2. Hermes: Wisdom that understands in silence [such is the matter and the womb from out which Man is born], and the True Good the seed.

Tat: Who is the sower, father? For I am altogether at a loss.

Hermes: It is the Will of God, my son.

Tat: And of what kind is he that is begotten, father? For I have no share of that essence in me, which doth transcend the senses. The one that is begot will be another one from God, God's Son?

Hermes: All in all, out of all powers composed.

Tat: Thou tellest me a riddle, father, and dost not speak as father unto son.

Hermes: This Race, my son, is never taught; but when He willeth it, its memory is restored by God.

3. Tat: Thou sayest things impossible, O

father, things that are forced. Hence answers would I have direct unto these things. Am I a son strange to my father's race?

Keep it not, father, back from me. I am a true-born son; explain to me the manner of Rebirth.

Hermes: What may I say, my son? I can but tell thee this. Whene'er I see within myself the Simple Vision brought to birth out of God's mercy, I have passed through myself into a Body that can never die. And now i am not as I was before; but I am born in Mind.

The way to do this is not taught, and it cannot be seen by the compounded element by means of which thou seest.

Yea, I have had my former composed form dismembered for me. I am no longer touched, but I have touch; I have dimension too; and [yet] am I a stranger to them now.

Thou seest me with eyes, my son; but what I am thou dost not understand [even] with fullest strain of body and of sight.

4. Tat: Into fierce frenzy and mind-fury hast

thou plunged me, father, for now no longer do I see myself.

Hermes: I would, my son, that thou hadst e'en passed right through thyself, as they who dream in sleep yet sleepless.

Tat: Tell me this too! Who is the author of Rebirth?

Hermes: The Son of God, the One Man, by God's Will.

5. Tat: Now hast thou brought me, father, unto pure stupefaction. Arrested from the senses which I had before,...<lacuna in original text>; for [now] I see thy Greatness identical with thy distinctive form.

Hermes: Even in this thou art untrue; the mortal form doth change with every day. 'Tis turned by time to growth and waning, as being an untrue thing.

6. Tat: What then is true, Thrice-greatest One?

Hermes: That which is never troubled, son, which cannot be defined; that which no color hath, nor any figure, which is not turned, which hath no garment, which giveth light; that which is comprehensible unto itself [alone], which doth not suffer change; that which no body can contain.

Tat: In very truth I lose my reason, father. Just when I thought to be made wise by thee, I find the senses of this mind of mine blocked up.

Hermes: Thus is it, son: That which is upward borne like fire, yet is borne down like earth, that which is moist like water, yet blows like air, how shalt thou this perceive with sense - the that which is not solid nor yet moist, which naught can bind or loose, of which in power and energy alone can man have any notion - and even then it wants a man who can perceive the Way of Birth in God?

7. Tat: I am incapable of this, O father, then?

Hermes: Nay, God forbid, my son! Withdraw into thyself, and it will come; will, and it comes to pass; throw out of work the body's senses, and thy Divinity shall come to birth; purge from thyself the brutish torments - things of matter.

Tat: I have tormentors then in me, O father?

Hermes: Ay, no few, my son; nay, fearful ones and manifold.

Tat: I do not know them, father.

Hermes: Torment the first is this Not-knowing, son; the second one is Grief; the third, Intemperance; the fourth, Concupiscence; the fifth, Unrighteousness; the sixth is Avarice; the seventh, Error; the eighth is Envy; the ninth, Guile; the tenth is Anger; eleventh, Rashness; the twelfth is Malice.

These are in number twelve; but under them are many more, my son; and creeping through the prison of the body they force the man that's placed therein to suffer in his senses. But they depart (though not all at once) from him who hath been taken pity on by God; and this it is which constitutes the manner of Rebirth. And... <lacuna in the

original text> the Reason (Logos).

8. And now, my son, be still and solemn silence keep! Thus shall the mercy that flows on us from God not cease.

Henceforth rejoice, O son, for by the Powers of God thou art being purified for the articulation of the Reason (Logos).

Gnosis of God hath come to us, and when this comes, my son, Not-knowing is cast out.

Gnosis of Joy hath come to us, and on its coming, son, Sorrow will flee away to them who give it room. The Power that follows Joy do I invoke, thy Self-control. O Power most sweet! Let us most gladly bid it welcome, son! How with its coming doth it chase Intemperance away!

9. Now fourth, on Continence I call, the Power against Desire. <lacuna in the original text> This step, my son, is Righteousness' firm seat. For without judgement <other translators read this "without effort"> see how she hath chased Unrighteousness away. We

are made righteous, son, by the departure of Unrighteousness.

Power sixth I call to us - that against Avarice, Sharing-with-all.

And now that Avarice is gone, I call on Truth. And Error flees, and Truth is with us.

See how [the measure of] the Good is full, my son, upon Truth's coming. For Envy is gone from us; and unto Truth is joined the Good as well, with Life and Light.

And now no more doth any torment of the Darkness venture nigh, but vanquished [all] have fled with whirring wings.

10. Thou knowest [now], my son, the manner of Rebirth. And when the Ten is come, my son, that driveth out the Twelve, the Birth in understanding <literally "intellectual birth", **noera genesis**> is complete, and by this birth we are made into Gods.

Who then doth by His mercy gain this Birth in God, abandoning the body's senses, knows himself [to be of Light and Life] and that he doth consist of these, and [thus] is filled with bliss.

11. Tat: By God made steadfast, father, no longer with the sight my eyes afford I look on things, but with the energy the Mind doth give me through the Powers.

In Heaven am I, in earth, in water, air; I am in animals, in plants; I'm in the womb, before the womb, after the womb; I'm everywhere!

But further tell me this: How are the torments of the Darkness, when they are twelve in number, driven out by the ten Powers? What is the way of it, Thrice-greatest one?

12. Hermes: This dwelling-place through which we have just passed <i.e., the human body>, my son, is constituted from the circle of the twelve types-of-life, this being composed of elements, twelve in number, but of one nature, an omniform idea. For man's delusion there are disunions in them, son, while in their action they are one. Not only can we never part Rashness from Wrath; they cannot even be distinguished.

According to right reason (logos), then, they <the Twelve> naturally withdraw once and for all, in as much as they are chased out by no less than ten powers, that is, the Ten.

For, son, the Ten is that which giveth birth to souls. And Life and Light are unified there, where the One hath being from the Spirit. According then to reason (logos) the One contains the Ten, the Ten the One.

13. Tat: Father, I see the All, I see myself in Mind.

Hermes: This is, my son, Rebirth - no more to look on things from body's view-point (a thing three ways in space extended)... <lacuna in text>, though this Sermon (Logos) on Rebirth, on which I did not comment - in order that we may not be calumniators of the All unto the multitude, to whom indeed God Himself doth will we should not.

14. Tat: Tell me, O father: This Body which is made up of the Powers, is it at any time dissolved?

Hermes: Hush, [son]! Speak not of things impossible, else wilt thou sin and thy Mind's eye be quenched.

The natural body which our sense perceives is far removed from this essential birth.

The first must be dissolved, the last can never be; the first must die, the last death cannot touch.

Dost thou not know thou hast been born a God, Son of the One, even as I myself?

15. Tat: I would, O father, hear the Praise-giving with hymn which thou didst say thou heardest then when thou wert at the Eight [the Ogdoad] of Powers

Hermes: Just as the Shepherd did foretell [I should], my son, [when I came to] the Eight.

Well dost thou haste to "strike thy tent" <i.e., be free from the physical body>, for thou hast been made pure.

The Shepherd, Mind of all masterhood, hath not passed on to me more than hath been written down, for full well did he know that I should of myself be able to learn all, and hear what I should wish, and see all things.

He left to me the making of fair things; wherefore the Powers within me. e'en as they are in all, break into song.

16. Tat: Father, I wish to hear; I long to know these things.

Hermes: Be still, my son; hear the Praise-giving now that keeps [the soul] in tune, Hymn of Re-birth - a hymn I would not have thought fit so readily to tell, had'st thou not reached the end of all.

Wherefore this is not taught, but is kept hid in silence.

Thus then, my son, stand in a place uncovered to the sky, facing the southern wind, about the sinking of the setting sun, and make thy worship; so in like manner too when he doth rise, with face to the east wind.

Now, son, be still!

The Secret Hymnody

17. Let every nature of the World receive the utterance of my hymn!

Open thou Earth! Let every bolt of the Abyss be drawn for me. Stir not, ye Trees!

I am about to hymn creation's Lord, both All and One.

Ye Heavens open and ye Winds stay still; [and] let God's deathless Sphere receive my word (logos)!

For I will sing the praise of Him who founded all; who fixed the Earth, and hung up Heaven, and gave command that Ocean should afford sweet water [to the Earth], to both those parts that are inhabited and those that are not, for the support and use of every man; who made the Fire to shine for gods and men for every act.

Let us together all give praise to Him, sublime above the Heavens, of every nature Lord!

'Tis He who is the Eye of Mind; may He accept the praise of these my Powers!

18. Ye powers that are within me, hymn the One and All; sing with my Will, Powers all that are within me!

O blessed Gnosis, by thee illumined, hymning through thee the Light that mond alone can see, I joy in Joy of Mind.

Sing with me praises all ye Powers!

Sing praise, my Self-control; sing thou through me, my Righteousness, the praises of the Righteous; sing thou, my Sharing-all, the praises of the All; through me sing, Truth, Truth's praises!

Sing thou, O Good, the Good! O Life and Light, from us to you our praises flow!

Father, I give Thee thanks, to Thee Thou Energy of all my Powers; I give Thee thanks, O God, Thou Power of all my Energies!

19. Thy Reason (Logos) sings through me Thy praises. Take back through me the All into [Thy] Reason - [my] reasonable oblation!

Thus cry the Powers in me. They sing Thy praise, Thou All; they do Thy Will.

From Thee Thy Will; to Thee the All.

Receive from all their reasonable oblation. The All that is in us, O Life, preserve; O Light<,> illumine it; O God<,> in-spirit it.

It it Thy Mind that plays the shepherd to Thy Word, O Thou Creator, Bestower of the Spirit [upon all].

20. [For] Thou art God, Thy Man thus cries to Thee through Fire, through Air, through Earth, through Water, [and] through Spirit, through Thy creatures.

'Tis from Thy Aeon I have found praise-giving; and in thy Will, the object of my search, have I found rest.

Tat: By thy good pleasure have I seen this praise-giving being sung, O father; I have set it in my Cosmos too.

Hermes: Say in the Cosmos that thy mind alone can see, my son.

Tat: Yea, father, in the Cosmos that the mind alone can see; for I have been made able by thy Hymn, and by thy Praise-giving my mind hath been illumined. But further I myself as well would from my natural mind send praise-giving to God.

21. Hermes: But not unheedfully, my son.

Tat: Aye. What I behold in mind, that do I say.

To thee, thou Parent of my Bringing into Birth, as unto God I, Tat, send reasonable offerings. o God and Father, thou art the Lord, thou art the Mind. Receive from me oblations reasonable as thou would'st wish; for by thy Will all things have been perfected.

Hermes: Send thou oblation, son, acceptable to God, the Sire of all; but add, my son, too, "through the Word" (Logos).

Tat: I give thee, father, thanks for showing me to sing such hymns.

22. Hermes: Happy am I, my son, that though hast brought the good fruits forth of Truth, products that cannot die.

And now that thou hast learnt this lesson from me, make promise to keep silence on thy virtue, and to no soul, my son, make known the handing on to thee the manner of Rebirth, that we may not be thought to be calumniators.

And now we both of us have given heed sufficiently, both I the speaker and the hearer thou.

In Mind hast thou become a Knower of thyself and our [common] Sire.

A Letter of Thrice-Greatest
Hermes to Asclepius

UNTO ASCLEPIUS GOOD
HEALTH OF SOUL!

1. SINCE IN THY ABSENCE my son Tat desired to learn the nature of the things that are, and would not let me hold it over, as [natural to] a younger son fresh come to gnosis of the [teachings] on each single

169

point,—I was compelled to tell [him] more, in order that the contemplation [of them] might be the easier for him to follow.

I would, then, choosing out the chiefest heads of what was said, write them in brief to thee, explaining them more mystic-ly, as unto one of greater age and one well versed in Nature.

2. If all things manifest have been and are being made, and made things are not made by their own selves but by another; [if] made things are the **many**,—nay more, are **all** things manifest and all things different and not alike; and things that are being made are being made by other [than themselves];— there is some one who makes these things; and He cannot be made, but is more ancient than the things that can.

For things that can be made, I say, are made by other [than themselves]; but of the things that owe their being to their being made, it is impossible that anything should be more ancient than them all, save only

That which is not able to be made.

3. So He is both Supreme, and One, and Only, the truly wise in all, as having naught more ancient [than Himself].

For He doth rule o'er both the number, size and difference of things that are being made, and o'er the continuity of their making [too].

Again, things makeable are seeable; but He cannot be seen.

For for this cause He maketh,–that He may not be able to be seen.

He, therefore, ever maketh; and therefore can He ne'er be seen.

To comprehend Him thus is meet; and comprehending, [it is meet] to marvel; and marvelling, to count oneself as blessed, as having learnt to know one's Sire.

4. For what is sweeter than one's own true Sire? Who, then, is He; and how shall we learn how to know Him?

Is it not right to dedicate to Him alone the name of God, or that of Maker, or of Father, or rather [all] the three;–God for His Power, and Maker for His Energy, and Father for His Good?

Now Power doth differ from the things which are being made; while Energy consisteth in all things being made.

Wherefore we ought to put away verbosity and foolish talk, and understand these two— the made and Maker. For that of them there is no middle [term]; there is no third.

5. Wherefore in all that thou conceivest, in all thou nearest, these two recall to mind; and think all things are they, reckoning as doubtful naught, nor of the things above, nor of the things below, neither of things divine, nor things that suffer change or things that are in obscuration.

For all things are [these] twain, Maker and made, and 'tis impossible that one should be without the other; for neither is it possible that "Maker" should exist without the "made," for each of them is one and the same thing.

Wherefore 'tis no more possible for one

from other to be parted, than self from self.

6. Now if the Maker is naught else but That which makes, Alone, Simple, Uncompound, it needs must do this [making] to Itself,– to Which its Maker's making is "its being made."

And as to all that's being made,–it cannot be

[so made] by being made by its own self; but it must needs be made by being made by other. Without the "Maker" "made" is neither made nor is; for that the one without the other doth lose its proper nature by deprivation of that other.

If, then, all things have been admitted to be two,–the "that which is being made" and "that which makes,"–[all then] are one in union of these,–the "that which leadeth" and the "that which followeth."

The making God is "that which leadeth"; the "that which is being made," whatever it be, the "that which followeth."

7. And do not thou be chary of things

made because of their variety, from fear of attribution of a low estate and lack of glory unto God.

For that His Glory's one,—to make all things; and this is as it were God's Body, the making [of them].

But by the Maker's self naught is there thought or bad or base.

These things are passions which accompany the making process, as rust doth brass and filth doth body; but neither doth the brass-smith make the rust, nor the begetters of the body filth, nor God [make] evil.

It is continuance in the state of being made 1 that makes them lose, as though it were, their bloom; and 'tis because of this God hath made change, as though it were the making clean of genesis.

8. Is it, then, possible for one and the same painter man to make both heaven, and gods, and earth, and sea, and men, and all the animals, and lifeless things,

and trees, and yet impossible for God to make all things?

What monstraus lack of understanding; what want of knowledge as to God!

For such the strangest lot of all do suffer; for though they say they worship piously and sing the praise of God, yet by their not ascribing unto Him the making of all things, they know not God; and, added unto this not-knowing, they're guilty even of the worst impiety to Him—passions to Him attributing, or arrogance, or impotency.

For if He doth not make all things, from arrogance He doth not make, or not being able,—which is impiety [to think].

9. One Passion hath God only—Good; and He who's Good, is neither arrogant nor impotent.

For this is God—the Good, which hath all power of making all.

And all that can be made is made by God,— that is, by [Him who is] the Good and who can make all things.

But would'st thou learn how He doth make, and how things made are made, thou may'st do so.

10. Behold a very fair and most resemblant image—a husbandman casting the seed into the ground; here wheat, there barley, and there [again] some other of the seeds!

Behold one and the same man planting the vine, the apple, and [all] other trees!

In just the selfsame way doth God sow Immortality in Heaven, and Change on Earth, and Life and Motion in the universe.

These are not many, but few and easy to be numbered; for four in all are they,—and God Himself and Genesis, in whom are all that are.

CHAPTER SIXTEEN

The Definitions of Asclepius unto King Ammon

THE PERFECT SERMON OF ASCLEPIUS UNTO THE KING

1. GREAT IS THE SERMON (**logos**) which I send to thee, O King—the summing up and digest, as it were, of all the rest.

For it is not composed to suit the many's prejudice, since it contains much that

177

refuteth them.

Nay, it will seem to thee as well to contradict sometimes my sermons too.

Hermes, my master, in many a conversation, both when alone, and sometimes, too, when Tat was there, has said, that unto those who come across my books, their composition will seem most simple and [most] clear; but, on the contrary, as 'tis unclear, and has the [inner] meaning of its words concealed, it will be still unclearer, when, afterwards, the Greeks will want to turn our tongue into their own,–for this will be a very great distorting and obscuring of [even] what has been [already] written.

2. Turned into our own native tongue, the sermon (**logos**) keepeth clear the meaning of the words (**logoi**) [at any rate].

For that its very quality of sound, the [very] power of the Egyptian names, have in themselves the bringing into act of what is said.

As far as, then, thou canst, O King–(and

thou canst [do] all things)–keep [this] our sermon from translation; in order that such mighty mysteries may not come to the Greeks, and the disdainful speech of Greece, with [all] its looseness, and its surface beauty, so to speak, take all the strength out of the solemn and the strong– the energetic speech of Names.

The Greeks, O King, have novel words, energic of "argumentation" [only]; and thus is the philosophizing of the Greeks–the noise of words.

But we do not use words; but we use sounds full-filled with deeds.

3. Thus, then, will I begin the sermon by invocation unto God, the universals' Lord and Maker, [their] Sire, and [their] Encompasser; who though being All is One, and though being One is All; for that the Fullness of all things is One, and [is] in One, this latter One not coming as a second [One], but both being One.

And this is the idea that I would have

thee keep, through the whole study of our sermon, Sire!

For should one try to separate what **seems** to be both All **and** One **and** Same from One,–he will be found to take his epithet of "All" from [the idea of] multitude, and not from [that of) fullness–which is impossible; for if he part All from the One, he will destroy the All.

For all things **must** be One–if they indeed **are** One. Yea, they are One; and they shall never cease being One–in order that the Fullness may not be destroyed.

* * * * *

4. See then in Earth a host of founts of Water and of Fire forth-spirting in its midmost parts; in one and the same [space all] the three natures visible–of Fire, and Water, and of Earth, depending from one Root.

Whence, too, it is believed to be the Treasury of every matter. It sendeth forth of its abundance, and in the place [of what it sendeth forth] receiveth the subsistence from above.

For thus the Demiurge—I mean the Sun—eternally doth order Heaven and Earth, pouring down Essence, and taking Matter up, drawing both round Himself and to Himself all things, and from Himself giving all things to all.

For He it is whose goodly energies extend not only through the Heaven and the Air, but also onto Earth, right down unto the lowest Depth and the Abyss.

6. And if there be an Essence which the mind alone can grasp, this is his Substance, the reservoir of which would be His Light.

But whence this [Substance] doth arise, or floweth forth, He, [and He] only, knows.

*   *   *   *   *

Or rather, in space and nature, He is near unto Himself . . . though as He is not seen by us, . . . understand [Him] by conjecture.

7. The spectacle of Him, however, is not left unto conjecture; nay [for] His very rays, in greatest splendour, shine all round on

all the Cosmos that doth lie above and lie below.

For He is stablished in the midst, wreathed with the Cosmos, and just as a good charioteer, He safely drives the cosmic team, and holds them in unto Himself, lest they should run away in dire disorder.

The reins are Life, and Soul, and Spirit, Deathlessness, and Genesis.

He lets it, then, drive [round] not far off from Himself—nay, if the truth be said, together with Himself.

8. And in this way He operates all things. To the immortals He distributeth perpetual permanence; and with the upper hemisphere of His own Light—all that he sends above from out His other side, [the side of him] which looks to Heaven—He nourisheth the deathless parts of Cosmos.

But with that side that sendeth down [its Light], and shineth round all of the hemisphere of Water, and of Earth, and Air, He vivifieth, and by births and changes keepeth in movement to and fro the animals in these [the lower] parts of Cosmos. . . .

9. He changes them in spiral fashion, and doth transform them into one another, genus to genus, species into species, their mutual changes into one another being balanced– just as He does when He doth deal with the Great Bodies.

For in the case of every body, [its] permanence [consists in] transformation.

In case of an immortal one, there is no dissolution; but when it is a mortal one, it is accompanied with dissolution.

And this is how the deathless body doth differ from the mortal, and how the mortal one doth differ from the deathless.

10. Moreover, as His Light's continuous, so is His Power of giving Life to lives continuous, and not to be brought to an end in space or in abundance.

For there are many choirs of daimons round Him, like unto hosts of very various kinds; who though they dwell with mortals, yet are not far from the immortals; but having as their lot from here unto the spaces of the Gods, they watch o'er the affairs of men, and work out things appointed by the Gods–by means of storms, whirlwinds and hurricanes, by transmutations wrought by fire and shakings of the earth, with famines also and with wars requiting [man's] impiety,–for this is in man's case the greatest ill against the Gods.

11. For that the duty of the Gods is to give benefits; the duty of mankind is to give worship; the duty of the daimons is to give requital.

For as to all the other things men do, through error, or foolhardiness, or by necessity, which they call Fate, or ignorance–these are not held requitable among the Gods; impiety alone is guilty at their bar.

12. The Sun is the preserver and the nurse of every class.

And just as the Intelligible World, holding the Sensible in its embrace, fills it [all] full, distending it with forms of every kind and every shape–so, too, the Sun distendeth all in Cosmos, affording births to all, and strengtheneth them.

When they are weary or they fail, He takes them in His arms again.

13. And under Him is ranged the choir of daimons–or, rather, choirs; for these are multitudinous and very varied, ranked underneath the groups of Stars, in equal number with each one of them.

So, marshalled in their ranks, they are the ministers of each one of the Stars, being in their natures good, and bad, that is, in their activities (for that a daimon's essence is activity); while some of them are [of] mixed [natures], good and bad.

14. To all of these has been allotted the authority o'er things upon the Earth; and it is they who bring about the multifold confusion of the turmoils on the Earth–for states and nations generally, and for each individual separately.

For they do shape our souls like to themselves, and set them moving with them,—obsessing nerves, and marrow, veins and arteries, the brain itself, down to the very heart.

15. For on each one of us being born and made alive, the daimons take hold on us—those [daimones] who are in service at that moment [of the wheel] of Genesis, who are ranged under each one of the Stars.

For that these change at every moment; they do not stay the same, but circle back again.

These, then, descending through the body to the two parts of the soul, set it awhirling, each one towards its own activity.

But the soul's rational part is set above the lordship of the daimons—designed to be receptacle of God.

16. Who then doth have a Ray shining upon him through the Sun within his rational part—and these in all are few on them

the daimons do not act; for no one of the daimons or of Gods has any power against one Ray of God.

As for the rest, they are all led and driven, soul and body, by the daimons—loving and hating the activities of these.

The reason (**logos**), [then,] is not the love that is deceived and that deceives.

The daimons, therefore, exercise the whole of this terrene economy, using our bodies as [their] instruments.

And this economy Hermes has called Heimarmenē.

17. The World Intelligible, then, depends from God; the Sensible from the Intelligible [World].

The Sun, through the Intelligible and the Sensible Cosmos, pours forth abundantly the stream from God of Good,—that is, the demiurgic operation.

And round the Sun are the Eight Spheres, dependent from Him—the [Sphere] of the Non-wandering Ones, the Six [Spheres] of the Wanderers, and one Circumterrene.

And from the Spheres depend the daimones; and from these, men.

And thus all things and all [of them] depend from God.

18. Wherefore God is the Sire of all; the Sun's [their] Demiurge; the Cosmos is the instrument of demiurgic operation.

Intelligible Essence regulateth Heaven; and Heaven, the Gods; the daimones, ranked underneath the Gods, regulate men.

This is the host of Gods and daimones.

Through these God makes all things for His own self.

And all [of them] are parts of God; and if they all [are] parts–then, God is all.

Thus, making all, He makes Himself; nor ever can He cease [His making], for He Himself is ceaseless.

Just, then, as God doth have no end and no beginning, so doth His making have no end and no beginning.

*   *   *   *   *

CHAPTER SEVENTEEN

Of Asclepius to the King

ASCLEPIUS. IF THOU DOST THINK [of it], O King, even of bodies there are things bodiless.

The King. What [are they]?–(asked the King.)

Asc. The bodies that appear in mirrors– do they not seem then to have no body?

The King. It is so, O Asclepius; thou thinkest like a God!–(the King replied.)

Asc. There are things bodiless as well as these; for instance, forms—do not they seem to thee to have no body, but to appear in bodies not only of the things which are ensouled, but also of those which are not ensouled?

The King. Thou sayest well, Asclepius.

Asc. Thus, [then,] there are reflexions of things bodiless on bodies, and of bodies too upon things bodiless—that is to say, [reflexions] of the Sensible on the Intelligible World, and of the [World] Intelligible on the Sensible.

Wherefore, pay worship to the images, O King, since they too have their forms as from the World Intelligible.

(Thereon His Majesty arose and said:)

The King. It is the hour, O Prophet, to see about the comfort of our guests. To-morrow, [then,] will we resume our sacred converse.

CHAPTER EIGHTEEN

The Encomium of Kings

ABOUT THE SOUL'S BEING HINDERED BY THE PASSION OF THE BODY

1. [NOW] IN THE CASE of those professing the harmonious art of muse-like melody— if, when the piece is played, the discord of the instruments doth hinder their intent, its rendering becomes ridiculous.

For when his instruments are quite too weak for what's required of them, the music-artist needs must be laughed at by the audience.

For He, with all good will, gives of His art unweariedly; they blame the [artist's] weakness.

He then who is the Natural Musician-God, not only in His making of the harmony of His [celestial] songs, but also in His sending forth the rhythm of the melody of His own song[s] right down unto the separate instruments, is, as God, never wearied.

For that with God there is no growing weary.

2. So, then, if ever a musician desires to enter into the highest contest of his art he can—when now the trumpeters have rendered the same phrase of the [composer's] skill, and afterwards the flautists played the sweet notes of the melody upon their instruments, and they complete the music of the piece with pipe and plectrum—[if any thing goes wrong,] one does not lay the blame upon the inspiration of the music-maker.

Nay, [by no means,]—to him one renders

the respect that is his due; one blames the falseness of the instrument, in that it has become a hindrance to those who are most excellent–embarrassing the maker of the music in [the execution of] his melody, and robbing those who listen of the sweetness of the song.

3. In like way also, in our case, let no one of our audience for the weakness that inheres in body, blame impiously our Race.

Nay, let him know God is Unwearied Spirit– for ever in the self-same way possessed of His own science, unceasing in His joyous gifts, the self-same benefits bestowing everywhere.

4. And if the Pheidias–the Demiurge–is not responded to, by lack of matter to perfect His skilfulness, although for His own part the Artist has done all he can, let us not lay the blame on Him.

But let us, [rather,] blame the weakness of the string, in that, because it is too slack or is too tight, it mars the rhythm of the harmony.

5. So when it is that the mischance occurs by reason of the instrument, no one doth blame the Artist.

Nay, [more;] the worse the instrument doth chance to be, the more the Artist gains in reputation by the frequency with which his hand doth strike the proper note, and more the love the listeners pour upon that Music-maker, without the slightest thought of blaming him.

So will we too, most noble [Sirs], set our own lyre in tune again, within, with the Musician!

6. Nay, I have seen one of the artist-folk— although he had no power of playing on the lyre—when once he had been trained for the right noble theme, make frequent use of his own self as instrument, and tune the service of his string by means of mysteries, so that the listeners were amazed at how he turned necessitude into magnificence.

Of course you know the story of the harper who won the favour of the God who is the president of music-work.

[One day,] when he was playing for a prize, and when the breaking of a string became a hindrance to him in the contest, the favour of the Better One supplied him with another string, and placed within his grasp the boon of fame.

A grasshopper was made to settle on his lyre, through the foreknowledge of the Better One, and [so] fill in the melody in substitution of the [broken] string.

And so by mending of his string the harper's grief was stayed, and fame of victory was won.

7. And this I feel is my own case, most noble [Sirs]!

For but just now I seemed to make confession of my want of strength, and play the weakling for a little while; but now, by virtue of the strength of [that] Superior One, as though my song about the King had been perfected [by Him, I seem] to wake my muse.

For, you must know, the end of [this] our

duty will be the glorious fame of Kings, and the good-will of our discourse (**logos**) [will occupy itself] about the triumphs which they win.

Come then, let us make haste! For that the singer willeth it, and hath attuned his lyre 2 for this; nay more, more sweetly will he play, more fitly will he sing, as he has for his song the greater subjects of his theme.

8. Since, then, he has the [stringing] of his lyre tuned specially to Kings, and has the key of laudatory songs, and as his goal the Royal praises, let him first raise himself unto the highest King–the God of wholes.

Beginning, [then,] his song from the above, he, [thus,] in second place, descends to those after His likeness who hold the sceptre's power; since Kings themselves, indeed, prefer the [topics] of the song should step by step descend from the above, and where they have their [gifts of] victory presided o'er for them, thence should their hopes be led in orderly succession.

9. Let, then, the singer start with God, the greatest King of wholes, who is for ever free from death, both everlasting and possessed of [all] the might of everlastingness, the Glorious Victor, the very first, from whom all victories descend to those who in succession do succeed to victory.

10. Our sermon (**logos**) then, doth hasten to descend to [Kingly] praises and to the Presidents of common weal and peace, the Kings—whose lordship in most ancient times was placed upon the highest pinnacle by God Supreme; for whom the prizes have already been prepared even before their prowess in the war; of whom the trophies have been raised even before the shock of conflict.

For whom it is appointed not only to be Kings but also to be best.

At whom, before they even stir, the foreign land doth quake.

* * * * *

(ABOUT THE BLESSING OF THE BETTER [ONE] AND PRAISING OF THE KING)

11. But now our theme (**logos**) doth hasten on to blend its end with its beginnings—with blessing of the Better [One]; and then to make a final end of its discourse (**logos**) on those divinest Kings who give us the [great] prize of peace.

For just as we began [by treating] of the Better [One] and of the Power Above, so let us make the end bend round again unto the same—the Better [One].

Just as the Sun, the nurse of all the things that grow, on his first rising, gathers unto himself the first-fruits of their yield with his most mighty hands, using his rays as though it were for plucking off their fruits—yea, [for] his rays are [truly] hands for him who plucketh first the most ambrosial [essences] of plants—so, too, should we, beginning from the Better [One], and [thus] recipient of His wisdom's stream, and turning it upon the garden of our souls above the heavens,—we should [direct and] train these [streams] of blessing back again unto their source, [blessing] whose entire power of germination [in us] He hath Himself poured into us.

12. 'Tis fit ten thousand tongues and voices should be used to send His blessings back again unto the all-pure God, who is the Father of our souls; and though we cannot utter what is fit—for we are [far] unequal to the task—[yet will we say what best we can].

For Babes just born have not the strength to sing their Father's glory as it should be sung; but they give proper thanks for them, according to their strength, and meet with pardon for their feebleness.

Nay, it is rather that God's glory doth consist in this [one] very thing—that He is greater than His children; and that the prelude and the source, the middle and the end, of blessings, is to confess the Father to be infinitely puissant and never knowing what a limit means.

13. So is it, too, in the King's case.

For that we men, as though we were the children of the King, feel it our natural duty to give praise to him. Still must we ask for pardon [for our insufficiency], e'en though 'tis granted by our Sire before we [even] ask.

And as it cannot be the Sire will turn from Babes new-born because they are so weak, but rather will rejoice when they begin to recognise [his love]—so also will the Gnosis of the all [rejoice], which doth distribute life to all, and power of giving blessing back to God, which He hath given [us].

14. For God, being Good, and having in Himself eternally the limit of His own eternal fitness, and being deathless, and containing in Himself that lot of that inheritance that cannot come unto an end, and [thus] for ever ever-flowing from out that energy of

His, He doth send tidings to this world down here [to urge us] to the rendering of praise that brings us home again.

With Him, therefore, is there no difference with one another; there is no partiality with Him.

But they are one in Thought. One is the Prescience of all. They have one Mind—their Father.

One is the Sense that's active through them—their passion for each other. 'Tis Love Himself who worketh the one harmony of all.

15. Thus, therefore, let us sing the praise of God.

Nay, rather, let us [first] descend to those who have received their sceptres from Him.

For that we ought to make beginning with our Kings, and so by practising ourselves on them, accustom us to songs of praise, and train ourselves in pious service to the Better [One].

[We ought] to make the very first beginnings

of our exercise of praise begin from him, and through him exercise the practice [of our praise], that so there may be in us both the exercising of our piety towards God, and of our praise to Kings.

16. For that we ought to make return to them, in that they have extended the prosperity of such great peace to us.

It is the virtue of the King, nay, 'tis his name alone, that doth establish peace.

He has his name of King because he levelleth the summits of dissension with his smooth tread, and is the lord of reason (**logos**) that [makes] for peace.

And in as much, in sooth, as he hath made himself the natural protector of the kingdom which is not his native land, his very name [is made] the sign of peace.

For that, indeed, you know, the appellation of the King has frequently at once restrained the foe.

Nay, more, the very statues of the King are peaceful harbours for those most tempest-tossed.

The likeness of the King alone has to appear to win the victory, and to assure to all the citizens freedom from hurt and fear.

    *   *   *   *   *

The Perfect Sermon

OR THE ASCLEPIUS

(TEXT: THE GREEK ORIGINAL IS LOST, and only a Latin version remains to us. I use the text of Hildebrand (G. F.), **L. Apuleii Opera Omnia ex Fide Optimorum Codicum** (Leipzig, 1842), Pars II., pp. 279-334; but have very occasionally preferred the text in Patrizzi's **Nova de Universis Philosophia** (Venice, 1593), or of the Bipontine edition of Appuleius, **Lucii Apuleji Madaurensis Platonici**

Philosophi Opera (Biponti, 1788), pp. 285-325.)

I

1.   [I. M.] [**TRISMEGISTUS.**] GOD, O Asclepius, hath brought thee unto us that thou mayest hear a Godly sermon, a sermon such as well may seem of all the previous ones we've [either] uttered, or with which we've been inspired by the Divine, more Godly than the piety of [ordinary] faith.

If thou with eye of intellect shalt **see** this Word thou shalt in thy whole mind be filled quite full of all things good.

If that, indeed, the "many" be the "good," and not the "one," in which are "all." Indeed the difference between the two is found in their agreement,–"All" is of "One" or "One" is "All." So closely bound is each to other, that neither can be parted from its mate.

But this with diligent attention shalt thou learn from out the sermon that shall follow

[this].

But do thou, O Asclepius, go forth a moment and call in the one who is to hear.

(And when he had come in, Asclepius proposed that Ammon too should be allowed to come. Thereon Thrice-greatest said:)

[**Tris.**] There is no cause why Ammon should be kept away from us. For we remember how we have ourselves set down in writing many things to his address, as though unto a son most dear and most beloved, of physics many things, of ethics [too] as many as could be.

It is, however, with **thy** name I will inscribe this treatise.

But call, I prithee, no one else but Ammon, lest a most pious sermon on a so great theme be spoilt by the admission of the multitude.

For 'tis the mark of an unpious mind to publish to the knowledge of the crowd a tractate brimming o'er with the full Greatness of Divinity.

(When Ammon too had come within the

holy place, and when the sacred group of four was now complete with piety and with God's goodly presence–to them, sunk in fit silence reverently, their souls and minds pendent on Hermes' lips, thus Love Divine began to speak.)

II

1. [**TRIS.**] THE SOUL of every man, O [my] Asclepius, is deathless; yet not all in like fashion, but some in one way or [one] time, some in another.

Asc. Is not, then, O Thrice-greatest one, each soul of one [and the same] quality?

Tris. How quickly hast thou fallen, O Asclepius, from reason's true sobriety!

Did not I say that "All" is "One," and "One" is "All," in as much as all things have been in the Creator before they were created. Nor is He called unfitly "All," in that His members are the "All."

Therefore, in all this argument, see that

thou keep in mind Him who is "One"-"All," or who Himself is maker of the "All."

2. All things descend from Heaven to Earth, to Water and to Air.

'Tis Fire alone, in that it is borne upwards, giveth life; that which [is carried] downwards [is] subservient to Fire.

Further, whatever doth descend from the above, begetteth; what floweth upwards, nourisheth.

'Tis Earth alone, in that it resteth on itself, that is Receiver of all things, and [also] the Restorer of all genera that it receives.

This Whole, therefore, as thou rememberest, in that it is of all,—in other words, all things, embraced by nature under "Soul" and "World," are in [perpetual] flux, so varied by the multiform equality of all their forms, that countless kinds of well-distinguished qualities may be discerned, yet with this bond of union, that all should seem as One, and from "One" "All."

III

1. THAT, THEN, from which the whole Cosmos is formed, consisteth of Four Elements–Fire, Water, Earth, and Air; Cosmos [itself is] one, [its] Soul [is] one, and God is one.

Now lend to me the whole of thee,–all that thou can'st in mind, all that thou skill'st in penetration.

For that the Reason of Divinity may not be known except by an intention of the senses like to it.

'Tis likest to the torrent's flood, down-dashing headlong from above with all-devouring tide; so that it comes about, that by the swiftness of its speed it is too quick for our attention, not only for the hearers, but also for the very teachers.

GT GRANDTYPECLASSICS.COM

"There is no friend as loyal as a book." E. Hemingway

1984 BY G. ORWELL

20,000 Leagues Under the Sea BY J. VERNE

A Christmas Carol BY C. DICKENS

A Doll's House BY H. IBSEN

A Hero of Our Time BY M. LERMONTOV

A Little Princess BY F. H. BURNETT

A Passage to India BY E. M. FORSTER

A Room with a View BY E. M. FORSTER

A Study in Scarlet BY A. C. DOYLE

A Tale of Two Cities BY C. DICKENS

Aesop's Fables BY AESOP

Alice in Wonderland BY L. CARROLL

Animal Farm BY G. ORWELL

Anna Karenina BY L. TOLSTOY

Anne of Green Gables BY L. M. MONTGOMERY

Anthem BY A. RAND

As a Man Thinketh BY J. ALLEN

Autobiography of a Yogi BY P. YOGANANDA

Beyond Good and Evil BY F. NIETZSCHE

Black Beauty BY A. SEWELL

Bleak House BY C. DICKENS

Candide BY VOLTAIRE

Common Sense BY T. PAINE

Cranford by E. Gaskell

Crime and Punishment by F. Dostoevsky

David Copperfield by C. Dickens

Dead Souls by N. Gogol

Devils by F. Dostoevsky

Dombey and Son by C. Dickens

Don Quixote by M. de Cervantes

Dracula by B. Stoker

Dubliners by J. Joyce

Eugene Onegin by A. Pushkin

Far from the Madding Crowd by T. Hardy

Fathers and Sons by I. Turgenev

Fear and Trembling by S. Kierkegaard

Five Children and It by E. Nesbit

Flatland by E. A. Abbott

Frankenstein by M. Shelley

Gargantua and Pantagruel by F. Rabelais

Gone with the Wind by M. Mitchell

Gorgias by Plato

Great Expectations by C. Dickens

Grimm's Fairy Tales by J. and W. Grimm

Gulliver's Travels by J. Swift

And many more...

www.ingramcontent.com/pod-product-compliance
Lightning Source LLC
Chambersburg PA
CBHW020443100426
42812CB00036B/3427/J